35,00

D1402105

Al Sharpton

CIVIL RIGHTS LEADER

Black Americans of Achievement

LEGACY EDITION

Muhammad Ali	Spike Lee
Maya Angelou	Malcolm X
Louis Armstrong	Bob Marley
Josephine Baker	Thurgood Marshall
George Washington Carver	Eddie Murphy
Ray Charles	Barack Obama
Johnnie Cochran	Jesse Owens
Bill Cosby	Rosa Parks
Frederick Douglass	Colin Powell
W.E.B. Du Bois	Condoleezza Rice
Jamie Foxx	Paul Robeson
Aretha Franklin	Chris Rock
Marcus Garvey	Al Sharpton
Savion Glover	Will Smith
Alex Haley	Clarence Thomas
Jimi Hendrix	Sojourner Truth
Gregory Hines	Harriet Tubman
Billie Holiday	Nat Turner
Langston Hughes	Madam C.J. Walker
Jesse Jackson	Booker T. Washington
Magic Johnson	Oprah Winfrey
Scott Joplin	Stevie Wonder
Coretta Scott King	Tiger Woods
Martin Luther King Jr.	

Black Americans of Achievement

LEGACY EDITION

Al Sharpton

CIVIL RIGHTS LEADER

Wayne D'Orio

CHELSEA HOUSE
An Infobase Learning Company

Chelsea House
An imprint of Infobase Learning
132 West 31st Street
New York, NY 10001

Library of Congress Cataloging-in-Publication Data

D'Orio, Wayne.
  Reverend Al Sharpton: civil rights leader / Wayne D'Orio.
    p. cm. — (Black Americans of achievement, legacy edition)
  Includes bibliographical references and index.
  ISBN 978-1-60413-834-4 (hardcover)
  1. Sharpton, Al. 2. African Americans—Biography—Juvenile literature. 3. African American political activists—Biography—Juvenile literature. 4. African American civil rights workers—Biography—Juvenile literature. 5. African American clergy—New York (State)—New York—Biography—Juvenile literature. 6. African American politicians—New York (State)—New York—Biography—Juvenile literature. 7. New York (N.Y.)—Biography—Juvenile literature. I. Title. II. Series.
  E185.97.S54D67 2011
  973.92092—dc22 [B]   2010026886

Chelsea House books are available at special discounts when purchased in bulk quantities for businesses, associations, institutions, or sales promotions. Please call our Special Sales Department in New York at (212) 967-8800 or (800) 322-8755.

You can find Chelsea House on the World Wide Web at http://www.chelseahouse.com.

Text design by Keith Trego
Cover design by Keith Trego
Composition by Bill Brunson
Cover printed by Bang Printing, Brainerd, MN
Book printed and bound by Bang Printing, Brainerd, MN
Date printed: February 2011
Printed in the United States of America

10 9 8 7 6 5 4 3 2 1

This book is printed on acid-free paper.

All links and Web addresses were checked and verified to be correct at the time of publication. Because of the dynamic nature of the Web, some addresses and links may have changed since publication and may no longer be valid.

Contents

Loved and Hated,
But Always Out Front

On this day in January 2010, the Reverend Al Sharpton sits at the corner table at 540 Park, one of the most exclusive restaurants at one of the swankiest addresses in New York City, Park Avenue. In front of him are a pad and pen, his cell phone, and a BlackBerry. During our interview, friends and well wishers stop by his table to visit, and from his perch—his regular power-broker spot—he can survey all that happens in the room.

This morning he has already been to the NBC News studio to be interviewed about the hot topic of the day, Senate Majority Leader Harry Reid's comments on President Barack Obama. (Reid, quoted in a book about the 2008 election, *Game Change*, said Obama the candidate could be successful, in part, because he is "light-skinned.") He will be going back for another appearance in a half hour, but will have to decline his third invitation, because by that time, 1 P.M., he will kick off his syndicated radio show that takes him into 40 markets each day. His phone rings frequently, while his BlackBerry automatically captures a news feed of every story in which he is mentioned.

As his driver navigates the city, ferrying him to NBC at 30 Rockefeller Plaza, Sharpton works on his upcoming travel plans. He is due in England for a series of speeches, but wants to get back to the States in time for dinner with U.S. Education Secretary Arne Duncan the night before both are scheduled to be at an event in Atlanta. Sharpton arrives at NBC through a side door, quickly goes through security, and makes a short stop in the makeup room. Minutes later, he is sitting in the studio, awaiting questions from the host of an MSNBC show. Two minutes and four questions later, he is finished, down the hall, back into his car, and over to the studio where he conducts his radio show every day.

"I'm probably more disturbed when I'm not busy," he says, explaining how he thrives on the hectic pace. "I'm used to 18-hour workdays, five hours sleep, constantly moving. I go stir crazy when I'm not moving around." He recounts a recent four-day vacation to Bermuda with some childhood friends. Thanks to modern technology, he was able to conduct his typical Sunday sermon and host his daily radio show, much to the chagrin of his friends. "They gave up on me, said I was hopeless," he says with a laugh. "That's vacation for me."

THE RISE OF AL SHARPTON

How did Al Sharpton reach this perch? How did a boy preacher turn himself into one of the most well-known civil rights leaders of the past 25 years? How did he manage to turn around his image, from jogging suits and bombastic pronouncements, to fitted suits and a lower-key approach, all while never leaving the public eye?

If you wanted a quick look at the key civil rights events since 1985, you could crack open history books, click on search engines, or you could just study the life of the Rever-

Whenever a controversial news story happens, the Reverend Al Sharpton is often called on to comment on it. Here, Meredith Vieira of the NBC morning show *Today* interviews him on April 12, 2007, about some inflammatory comments made by radio personality Don Imus.

end Al Sharpton. From his social activism around the subway shooting of four black teenagers in 1984 to eulogizing Michael Jackson at his funeral in 2009, the Reverend Alfred Charles Sharpton Jr. has been front and center in the most heated civil rights cases, challenging authorities, organizing marches, drawing copious criticism, and according to him, standing up for the people who frequently have no voice.

Sharpton is one of the most divisive public figures in modern America. Many people feel he takes cases only for the publicity they bring him, while other opponents say he uses his power as an African-American leader to force corporations into consulting contracts or give donations to his organizations to avoid racial protests. His supporters tend to be less vocal, yet they participate in marches he organizes seemingly on a moment's notice, and in almost every case in which he has been involved, the victim's family has asked for his help. While the preacher is certainly one of the top civil rights leaders, his career is much more than just marches and protests: He has run for president and the U.S. Senate and hosts a three-hour radio show daily. He has also been arrested numerous times, nearly all on disorderly conduct charges, held a hunger strike, and was even stabbed once during a march he organized. He has visited Rwanda and Haiti, been a guest at the White House several times, and appeared on numerous national television shows. He has written two autobiographies, been featured on *60 Minutes*, and profiled in magazines too numerous to count. He has played himself in major motion pictures, been skewered repeatedly on *Saturday Night Live*, and appeared on more than 100 TV shows, including *The Daily Show with Jon Stewart*, *Larry King Live*, *The O'Reilly Factor*, *Real Time with Bill Maher*, and *Hannity & Colmes*. Typing his name into Google's search engine brings back 1.5 million hits in less than half a second.

NUMEROUS SUPPORTERS AND DETRACTORS

There is one exercise that shows how hard it can be to summarize the career of the Reverend Al Sharpton. Draw up a short list of his opponents and his supporters. Detractors include the Reverend Jesse Jackson; former New York City Mayor Ed Koch; former President Bill Clinton; former New York Governor Mario Cuomo; former House Speaker Newt Gingrich; founder of the Guardian Angels Curtis Sliwa; former Manhattan District Attorney Robert Morgantheau; and former U.S. Senator Daniel Patrick Moynihan.

Supporters include Michael Jackson, Jesse Jackson, Ed Koch, Newt Gingrich, James Brown, former Archbishop of New York

Cardinal John O'Connor, Howard Stern, and actress Susan Sarandon.

As the lists clearly show, Sharpton is at times at odds with the same people who later support his actions. Although Sharpton is a Democrat and has run for national office three times on the Democratic slate, his opponents are just as likely to include Democrats as Republicans. It is probably fair to say the smallest list you could make regarding Sharpton would be a list of people who either agree or disagree with every stand he has taken.

2

The Boy Preacher
Grows Up

Al Sharpton started following a long tradition of preachers before he could even spell the word, never mind appreciate the path he was taking. The early life of Sharpton is seldom mentioned when his work is debated, but several events during his childhood had a profound effect on his beliefs that remain to this day.

Alfred Charles Sharpton Jr. was born on October 3, 1954, in Brooklyn, New York, to Alfred Charles Sharpton Sr. and Ada Sharpton. He was raised in a middle-class home in Hollis, Queens, where his father ran his own store and both parents were landlords. Sharpton says he has no early memories, or first-hand experiences, involving whites. His earliest memories, in fact, revolve around the all-black Washington Temple Church of God in Christ, located at 37 Grant Square, near Prospect Park.

Sharpton attended the church with his family, including his sister. He says he can remember coming home at age three, lining up his sister's dolls, and preaching to them. The next year, Sharpton became a junior usher at the church, and when he was asked what he wanted to do to help celebrate the church's anniversary service, he knew exactly what to say. "I want to preach," he answered.

Of course, everyone laughed, but Sharpton's church adviser said the church's pastor, Bishop Frederick Douglas Washington, had started preaching when he was four. The adviser asked the bishop about the four-year-old Sharpton's request and he agreed to let the boy take the lectern. In his book *Go and Tell Pharaoh: The Autobiography of The Reverend Al Sharpton*, coauthored with Anthony Walton, Sharpton remembers his older half sister helping prepare him for the speech by typing up a manuscript. Even though he had yet to start school, Sharpton says, he read the sermon that weekend in front of the church's 900 members. He wrote: "I preached from the Gospel of John, the 14th chapter: 'Let not your heart be troubled: ye believe in God, believe also in me.' I remember being nervous. They had to put me on a box because I was too small for the pulpit and no one could see me."

At the age of 9 or 10, Sharpton was licensed and ordained as a Pentecostal minister by Bishop Washington. Sharpton recalled:

> I learned an awful lot from Bishop Washington. I learned how to preach, I learned how to love and respect books, I learned how to dress, I learned the persona of the black preacher, who is part religious leader, part social leader, part social worker, part entertainer. Through imitating people you admire, you learn things you don't come to understand until much later; you just do it.

(After Washington died in the late 1980s, Sharpton became a Baptist; when he was re-baptized by the Reverend William Jones at Bethany Baptist Church in 1994, he became a Baptist minister.)

A future religious leader and civil rights activist, Al Sharpton is seen here as a seven year old, preaching from a pulpit at Washington Temple in Brooklyn, New York, in 1961.

FAMILY UPHEAVAL

Right before Sharpton turned 10, his middle-class lifestyle changed drastically. His half sister, Ernestine, who everyone called Tina, admitted to having an affair with Al's father. (Tina was his mother's daughter from a marriage before she married Sharpton Sr.) Moreover, Tina was pregnant with Al's father's baby. When the revelation occurred, both she and his father moved out. In one fell swoop, Al lost his father, a sister, and the baby who would be both his younger brother and nephew (and was born looking just like Al).

Because Al and his mother also lost the family income, they were forced to move from Hollis, Queens, to the low-income housing projects in Brownsville, Brooklyn. His family went on welfare while his mother looked for work. When his mother filed for child support, his father countered that he should not have to pay because his son was earning money as a preacher. Sharpton says he was making money every week, but the amount could fluctuate from $10 to $100.

When the divorce was being heard in court, the judge in the case asked to see Al in his chambers. He ordered Al not to preach anymore and the young Sharpton agreed. When Friday came, however, he was preaching as usual. "That was the first time in my career that I defied a judge," Sharpton wrote in his book.

When the judge later asked him whether he had preached, Sharpton admitted he did. His answer surprised the judge, who asked whether his mother made him. He said she did not, and the judge asked why he did it then. "'Because I believe in what I'm doing.' And the judge turned to my father and said, 'Leave this kid alone.'"

THE CHARISMA OF ADAM CLAYTON POWELL

While his family life was undergoing many changes, young Al found a book that literally helped change the course of his professional life. When he was 11, he saw a book about Adam Clayton Powell Jr. and bought it for 99 cents. Though he later learned he was imitating people and following in black preachers' footsteps, this book was a revelation to him. He read it while riding the L subway train everyday, eventually becoming so enamored of Powell that he knew he had to go see him preach in person.

Lucky for Al, Powell preached in New York City, at Abyssinian Baptist Church in Harlem. With his sister along as a chaperone, Al took the subway to see Powell. He became mesmerized with everything about Powell. In his book, Sharpton said he liked the way Powell looked ("very tall," "striking," and "charismatic"), how he walked ("Adam had a way of not walking, but strutting, like a peacock"), how well he preached, and how the audience responded so enthusiastically to him.

After the service, Al went back to the pastor's office and asked a woman there if he could see Powell. After 10 minutes he could tell his message had not been delivered, so he asked again. "[She] came back out with a confused and sheepish look on her face. She waved to me and said, 'Follow me.'" Powell was shirtless in a room with two or three older women, but he knew Al by name and said he had listened to the radio broadcast (of Sharpton preaching) when he was in town. Powell asked him to go for a drink, and Sharpton was forced to remind him, "I'm 10, I don't drink." His new mentor said he would buy him a soda instead. At the bar, Powell got a scotch and held court. Sharpton wrote:

> It was the most incredible exhibition of power that I've ever seen, with people from every walk of life, including the top business and show and sports people that you'd see in the *Amsterdam News* and on TV, coming up to him one by one seeking favors or just to pay their respects, having little meetings and huddles with him all afternoon. I knew then what I wanted to be, that's when the other shoe dropped.

The boy preacher tried to stay close to Powell whenever he was in town, and often did so, following him to his appearance

One of Al Sharpton's mentors is the Reverend Jesse Jackson, a longtime religious and political leader, with whom he has always had a contentious relationship. Here, after a fight on the convention floor, Jackson addresses the 1972 Democratic Convention.

on *The David Frost Show*. Powell was flamboyant; he drove a Jaguar and toured Europe with two women—both beauty contest winners, one white and one black.

MEETING TWO MORE MENTORS

While Adam Clayton Powell had a big influence on the young Al's life, he was about to meet someone who would become a mentor, a rival, and finally a friend: Jesse Jackson.

After civil rights leader Reverend Martin Luther King Jr. was shot and killed on April 4, 1968, Al Sharpton—then 13—decided to join the civil rights movement by opening a youth division of Operation Breadbasket. This organization, started six years earlier, aimed to improve the economic conditions of African-American communities throughout the country. Jack-

The Godfather of Soul

Merging blues and gospel music with an ability to dance and play to the crowds like no one had seen before, James Brown became an American original through decades of performing. By the time of his death in December 2006, Brown was one of the most recognizable men in show business, famous for his flamboyant suits, his well-combed pompadour, his dance moves that would put a younger man in pain, his famous cape, and finally, his songs.

Brown started off following in the footsteps of Little Richard and Ray Charles, mixing gospel music with R&B while he sang with the group called The Flames. The band's first recording, "Please, Please, Please," hit number five on the R&B charts in 1956. Two years later, the group hit number one with the song "Try Me." Brown was so obviously the leader of the group at this time that the band was renamed James Brown and the Famous Flames.

In the early days of R&B, the single was all-important. Bands got radio play and concert bookings strictly on the strength of how far one song could go up the charts. Brown and his group were popular in the South, but had trouble selling records or getting shows outside of the region. With Brown footing the bill, he brought his band to New York City to play the famous Apollo Theater and record a live record. *Live at the Apollo* went to number

son, then 26, was the head of the Chicago branch, while King and others had been involved in the national group.

Jackson met young Al for the first time through this affiliation, and the older Jackson made an immediate impression on the teenager. Jackson was "young, brash, had a huge Afro, and wore a medallion," Sharpton remembers. Al immediately started wearing a medallion, and when the two got together, it wasn't long before Jackson was giving his protégé some advice: "Stay in school and don't be nobody's parrot."

Five years later, Al would meet the third man who would become a major mentor to him: James Brown. Unlike Powell and Jackson, Brown was not a preacher and did not hail from the civil rights movement. He was one of the most famous soul singers in the country, alternatively called the "Godfather of Soul" and "the hardest working man in show business."

two on the pop charts in 1963, staying on the charts for a full 14 months. The show captured the showman Brown was, including his oft-repeated trick of appearing to faint onstage only to be revived and continuing to perform as others were trying to bring him offstage to recover.

Two years later, Brown cut two of his biggest songs, "Papa's Got a Brand New Bag" and "I Got You (I Feel Good)"—both major R&B and pop hits. They also started Brown down a path he would remain on the rest of his life, using rhythm and horns to move R&B songs into a new type of music called funk.

Brown's music influenced a host of musicians, including a young Michael Jackson, who incorporated screams and scintillating dance moves into his performances with his family in the Jackson 5. In 1986, Brown was in the first class of inductees in the Rock and Roll Hall of Fame; *Rolling Stone* magazine ranked him as number seven on its list of 100 Greatest Artists of All Time in 2004. A road in his hometown of Augusta, Georgia, was renamed James Brown Way, and a full-size bronze statue was placed on the road.

When he died, several public and private services were held for Brown, including a show at the Apollo Theater in New York. The Reverend Al Sharpton officiated at each service.

In this circa-1981 photo, legendary entertainer James Brown departs from the White House in Washington, D.C., with the Reverend Al Sharpton. The two men had met with Vice President George H.W. Bush to advocate making Dr. Martin Luther King Jr.'s birthday a national holiday.

In the early 1970s, Al had become friends with Brown's son Teddy, when he came to New York City. After Teddy died in a car accident, James Brown came to the city and was introduced to Sharpton, who was roughly the same age as his son. He immediately became a mentor to Al, and said he wanted to play a benefit concert for the National Youth Movement, another organization Al was involved with. "I was awed," Sharpton remembers. "When I was a kid, I thought that when I'd seen Adam Clayton Powell I'd seen God, but after I saw James Brown, I knew I'd seen God." The next year Sharpton helped book Madison Square Garden when James Brown was having trouble reserving the famous venue. The concert ended up selling out. Brown made money and made sure that Sharpton's organization got money too.

As the two grew closer, Sharpton remembers Brown taking his preaching seriously and refused to let young Al come into some of the nightclubs where he performed, making him wait in his dressing room. He also refused to pay Al directly, instead making contributions to whatever charities the young man was involved with. "He didn't want me polluted by the entertainment world," Sharpton recalled. Brown told the young preacher, "I never want it said you worked in entertainment." Sharpton remembers Brown was "much stricter on me than anybody in my life."

Brown would also help to shape Sharpton's personal life in two significant ways. The first came through Al's role in helping the singer find backup singers. Brown used to audition singers on the road, using whatever concert he was playing that night to see if they could meet his demands. At one of his shows, one of the singers chosen for the band was Kathy Jordan from Niagara Falls, New York, who would later become Al Sharpton's wife.

"I don't know what happened between us; it just worked," Sharpton remembers. "I fell in love. She stood by me in some very rough times, which should be obvious to any observer. She left the band after we were married [in 1980] to come back to New York City with me, with no security." Sharpton and Jordan had two girls, before separating in 2004.

The second came in 1981, when Brown was invited to the White House to meet Vice President George Herbert Walker Bush to advocate for a national holiday to commemorate King's birthday. Brown invited Sharpton to come with him, even taking him to his personal hairdresser in Georgia. Brown told the hairdresser, "I want you to do the Reverend's hair like mine, because when we go to the White House, there's going to be a lot of press and when people see him, I want them to see me, like he's my son."

Although Sharpton would endure lots of jokes about his hair over the years, he had promised Brown to wear his hair like that until Brown died. Sharpton says that when Brown was jailed in the late 1980s, they would frequently talk by telephone, sometimes daily. "Even when he was in jail, he'd call me and say, 'Reverend, how's your hair?' And I'd say, 'Just like yours.'"

3

Hitting the National Stage

While Al Sharpton the preacher got an early start on one part of his profession, his rise as Al Sharpton the civil rights leader was slower. Sharpton had started protests and activism at the relatively early age of 14, but he did not garner any national attention until an event on the night of December 22, 1984, when the preacher was 30 years old.

The incident started under the streets in New York City, at a time when crime in major cities—and New York in particular—was at an all-time high. One white man and a group of four young African-American men ended up riding in the same subway car. When the young men twice asked Bernhard Goetz for $5, he claimed it was the beginning of a robbery. Goetz then pulled a loaded gun from his coat, stood up, fired five shots, and hit all four youths.

The entire event probably lasted less than 10 minutes, but the public reaction to the incident provoked strong reactions that lingered for years. Well before Goetz was arrested, a debate had begun to rage: Was Goetz justified in shooting these men because they were attempting to mug him? Was he a racist who unfairly perceived a threat because of the young men's race? How far should individuals be allowed to go in order to protect themselves? Other factors that made the Goetz case endlessly fascinating was the constantly changing information from all parties, the many trials convened in the case, and the lack of a clear resolution.

After the shootings, Goetz supposedly made sure that other riders in the car were not hurt. When the train conductor talked to him, Goetz said, "They tried to rob me," but he refused to turn over his gun, which he did not have a license to own. He then jumped out of the car, ran through the subway line, and ran back to the nearest station. Goetz then rented a car and drove to Vermont. Already the anonymous gunman was being called the "Subway Vigilante" by the city's tabloid newspapers. When it became obvious that the police were looking for him, Goetz surrendered to the police in Concord, New Hampshire, on New Year's Eve.

After Goetz was arrested, Manhattan District Attorney Robert Morgenthau convened a grand jury to hear the case—a type of jury used to determine whether criminal charges should be brought against a suspect. Morgenthau asked this group of 23 people to indict Goetz on a variety of charges, including four counts of attempted murder, four counts of assault, four counts of reckless endangerment, and criminal possession of a weapon. Neither Goetz nor the men who had been shot testified, but the grand jurors did consider police reports and hear from other witnesses. The grand jury then decided not to charge Goetz with any of the serious crimes, indicting him only on gun charges that would carry a year's sentence in jail if he were found guilty.

USING THE "CIVIL RIGHTS MANUAL"

Sharpton became a player in the case, but unlike many later civil rights issues, not the key player. Throughout all the case's twists, Sharpton and others kept the pressure on the authorities to charge Goetz with various crimes. His involvement in the case started as a reaction to some of the people and groups who cheered Goetz's actions. As he wrote in his first autobiography, "Everybody in the city seemed to treat [the shooting] as an act of heroism. I didn't see it that way. In fact, I thought it was crazy. The only thing that made these kids muggers rather than beggars was the color of their skin."

Sharpton called a news conference to denounce the situation, which in turn started a feud with Curtis Sliwa, the leader and organizer of the Guardian Angels. The Guardian Angels are a group of citizens who have banded together to patrol the city, offering residents more safety mostly through their presence.

After the first grand jury decision, Sharpton shifted his campaign into a higher gear. He started holding daily prayer vigils outside Goetz's home on Fourteenth Street, praying for the victims of the attack, one of whom was paralyzed after being shot in the spinal cord. "I learned those things from the Civil Rights manual, so to speak," Sharpton later wrote.

> Those techniques had never been used in New York before.... We created drama. That became my technique, to dramatize issues and events until something had to be done about it by the authorities. That's one of the things it means to be an activist in the media age. That means someone in authority, in the judicial system, has to answer.... We were the ones who agitated until [Goetz] was indicted on the gun charge.

Months later, a new police report surfaced, where Goetz told the officers that after he fired his first four shots, he looked at one of the young men, Darrell Cabey, then 19, who seemed unhurt and said, "You don't look so bad, here's another," then shot at him again. Cabey was paralyzed when a bullet severed his spinal cord. There is still debate about whether the extra shot Goetz fired missed Cabey or paralyzed him. Goetz later said he never uttered the infamous phrase before his last shot. At the time, several prominent people, including Sharpton and Governor Mario Cuomo of New York, called for a new trial.

Usually the law does not allow people to be tried more than once for the same incident, but because of the new information in the case, a second grand jury was convened. This time Goetz was charged with the more serious crimes—including attempted murder, assault, reckless endangerment, and several firearms offenses—and sent to a trial. He was acquitted of the more serious crimes, and again found guilty of only the gun charges. He was sentenced to a year in prison.

Sharpton called the verdict a "mixed blessing," unhappy with the ultimate punishment, but somewhat pleased with the way he was able to at least force Goetz to stand trial.

CENTER STAGE IN HOWARD BEACH

If the Goetz case was Sharpton's first supporting role on the national stage, the case in Howard Beach was his first turn at a starring one.

Late in 1986, three black men were driving in Howard Beach, a neighborhood in Queens, New York, when their car broke down. As they were walking to find a pay phone, an argument broke out with some white men. The three men ducked into a nearby pizzeria, but when they left 30 minutes later, the crowd was larger and people were shouting at them, with some calling them racial epithets. Some members of the crowd were armed with bricks and baseball bats.

When the three made it to the Belt Parkway, a major highway in the area, Michael Griffith, who was 24, tried to escape the crowd by crossing the highway. He was hit by a car and killed instantly. One of the other young men was beaten with bats and fists, while the third escaped without injury. Someone

In December 1986, the Reverend Al Sharpton leads a group of demonstrators through the Howard Beach neighborhood of Queens, New York, to protest the death of a young African-American man, Michael Griffith, who had tried to escape an angry white mob by crossing a highway.

who worked for Sharpton knew one of the families and asked him to get involved in the case. Sharpton went to Griffith's house, talked to his family, and called a news conference, during which he described the incident as a racial attack.

Looking to keep the issue in the media, Sharpton went back to the family's house and held another news conference, this time offering his own reward for information about the assailants. He then said he would hold a rally in front of the pizzeria the next day, in part to show residents of the area's mostly white residents that African Americans could safely travel anywhere in the city.

There was much uncertainty about what would happen at the rally. When the appointed time arrived, more than 100 cars were at the Griffith house ready to make the drive to the pizzeria. Sharpton wrote, "I was stunned.... This was extremely important to me personally, because it symbolized my transition from working with and leading young people to leading adults. I looked around and saw all those adults in their cars—ironically, I didn't own a car at the time—and I thought, I can do something."

A crowd of hundreds of angry whites, yelling racial epithets, met the motorcade. "It was just like the films I've seen of Mississippi in the sixties," Sharpton observed in his first autobiography, *Go and Tell Pharaoh*. He got out of the lead car and walked into the pizzeria with the crowd following him. In his speech, he said African Americans had fought too hard and come too far to be told where they could not go. In a move that highlighted both his quick thinking and his ability to rise to the moment, Sharpton took a $100 bill out of his pocket and ordered pizza for the crowd.

The event made the front page of the *New York Times* the next day. "We provided the occasion for the world to see the truth," the preacher wrote in *Go and Tell Pharaoh*.

Looking to keep the pressure on police and officials to arrest and convict the whites from the attack, Sharpton held another march a few days later, this time drawing 3,000 people and even more opposition. "Howard Beach was the beginning of me becoming for whites a symbol of hate and derision, and for blacks a symbol of standing up and going into these racist areas," Sharpton wrote in his first autobiography.

The district attorney in the case charged the several alleged attackers with reckless endangerment, outraging Sharpton and Griffith family lawyer Alton Maddox. As in the Goetz case, information was a key to public opinion. Because toxicology reports found that Griffith had cocaine in his body at the time of his death, some questioned whether that played a factor in his death. By keeping publicity about the case at center stage, Sharpton helped get a special prosecutor assigned to the case, which ended with five whites being indicted on charges of murder and manslaughter.

SHINING A LIGHT ON INJUSTICES

Besides thrusting Sharpton into the national consciousness, Howard Beach seemed to crystallize his thoughts on racism and his popularity with blacks. Unlike the South—where racial prejudice was overt and enshrined in Jim Crow laws that segregated the races and forced blacks to ride in the backs of buses, drink from separate water fountains, and attend different public schools—discrimination in the North, and particularly in big cities such as New York, was much subtler. Sharpton believes that the virulent opposition to his protests proved that racists existed in New York City and its suburbs.

"I think when people turned on the television, when we marched in Howard Beach and Bensonhurst, and saw people holding watermelons and calling people 'n-----s'—they never imagined that could happen in Brooklyn [or Queens]. If you had ... showed [people] tape of those marches, they would have thought it was Birmingham in '63 or Selma," Sharpton told *Salon*, referencing Alabama cities where anti-segregation marches by Martin Luther King Jr. and others faced violence. "No one would have believed it was New York.... The civil rights issues of the 1950s and 1960s never reached New York as a movement. The city sort of assumed this liberal image without ever going through the catharsis the South did."

When some members of the media accused Sharpton of being a media hound and only turning up for the cameras, he responded, as he recalled in *Go and Tell Pharaoh*:

I have been doing this since I was 14 years old, whether the cameras were there or not. There were no cameras at Tilden High School or the A&P [sites of his earliest protests], I wasn't in the paper, but I did the same thing every day: preach and agitate. I didn't do anything different at Howard Beach than I had always done. The difference was that it was on television and everybody could see me do it. And that was what was amazing to me about the media and how I was covered: nobody bothered to look up who I was

The History of the Civil Rights Movement

In 1954, the United States Supreme Court ruled that educating black children separately from whites was unconstitutional. The decision helped to spark the civil rights movement. In 1955, Rosa Parks became famous for refusing to move to the back of a bus in Montgomery, Alabama. A young Martin Luther King Jr. organized a boycott of the city's buses that lasted 381 days until the segregation rule was lifted.

The next big battle came in 1957, when nine black students sued to be admitted to Little Rock Central High School in Arkansas. Although they won the right to attend, Governor Orval Faubus used the National Guard to prevent the children from attending the school. President Dwight Eisenhower stepped in and used other soldiers to protect the African-American students when they went to the school. When the school year was over, the school system decided to shut its public schools rather than integrate, an action that was taken in other towns across the South.

From there, the events in the civil rights movement came faster: a sit-in at a segregated lunch counter in North Carolina; freedom rides to desegregate buses and bus terminals for interstate travel. The violence shown at many of these protests against blacks—including white students spitting at the Little Rock Nine, mass arrests at sit-ins, firebombed buses, and Ku Klux Klan members beating blacks involved in Alabama freedom rides—horrified much of the country.

King and other civil rights leaders had adopted the nonviolent protest and civil disobedience tactics that had been championed earlier by American author Henry David Thoreau and Mohandas Gandhi in India.

The year 1964 was a major one for the civil rights movement. King, then 35, became the youngest person ever to win the Nobel Peace Prize. Earlier that year, after overcoming 54 days of filibustering in Congress (a form of obstruction where one group attempts to delay a vote by extending debate), President Lyndon Johnson signed the Civil Rights Act. This not only banned

and what I had done. I thought I had a pretty consistent track record.

Sharpton's reputation as an advocate for African Americans, especially in cases where they are fighting authority figures, has endeared him to the black community in a way that many

discrimination based on race, color, religion, or country of origin, it also eliminated all state and local laws that required discrimination. In 1965, Congress passed the Voting Rights Act, which made it easier for Southern blacks to register to vote.

Martin Luther King Jr. addresses an overflow crowd at a mass meeting at the Holt Street Baptist Church. Just prior to this meeting, King was found guilty of conspiracy in the Montgomery bus boycott and fined $500. King vowed the boycott of city buses would continue.

whites still do not understand. He gets called in these incidents because he has proven the ability to focus the media's attention on an issue. While he certainly has not won every case, he has always managed to focus a light on a case and at least allow the people he represents to be heard.

4

Tawana Brawley

Mention the name Tawana Brawley to anyone who lived through 1987—particularly anyone who lived in New York City at the time—and odds are you will get a strong reaction. The case is so infamous that even more than 20 years later, with Brawley herself far out of the spotlight, it continues to be one of the defining events in Sharpton's career.

Why does this case still resonate when the details and emotions of other incidents have long been forgotten? Sharpton himself supplies the short answer:

> Tawana Brawley was the O.J. Simpson case before O.J. Simpson. You're into the murky swamp of taboo "race-mixing" and it all hit a nerve, a racial/sexual nerve, and it has nothing to do with whether anybody believed her or not.... If O.J.'s wife had been black, the soap operas would have been in full swing, and there would be no CNN, and

27

Mr. Simpson would be just another black man sitting up
in San Quentin.

He refers to O.J. Simpson, the black former football star who
was accused of murdering his white ex-wife and her friend in
1994. After a lengthy and highly publicized trial, often called
the "Trial of the Century" more than half the country watched
the verdict live on television. Simpson was acquitted of both
murder charges, although he was later found liable for their
wrongful deaths in a civil trial.

The long answer of why the Brawley case continues to
intrigue or upset people lies in the details. While some of the
incidents around the event remain in dispute all these years later,
this much is fact: on November 28, 1987, 15-year-old Tawana
Brawley was found in Dutchess County, about 60 miles (96.5
kilometers) north of Manhattan. She was lying in a garbage bag,
unresponsive. She said she had been raped by three and as many
as six white men in the nearby woods, with at least one of them
being a police officer. She had feces smeared across her body
and epithets written on her skin with something like charcoal.
Chunks of her hair had been pulled out by the roots. She had
been reported missing for four days before she was found.

The case generated an incredible amount of media attention. Her lawyers, Alton Maddox and C. Vernon Mason,
requested a special prosecutor because of the accusation
that the attack included a police officer. Even though the
lawyers got their request, with Governor Mario Cuomo
appointing New York State Attorney General Robert Abrams,
they advised Brawley not to speak with Abrams. A month after
the alleged attack, Sharpton became an adviser to the Brawley
family, joining the case when the family requested him, saying
they were unhappy with the efforts of the National Association
for the Advancement of Colored People (NAACP).

The case had many mysteries, including a note that Brawley
scribbled that read, "I want Scoralic. I want Scoralic dead."

On August 28, 1988, Tawana Brawley's chief advisers—C. Vernon Mason, *(second from left)*, Al Sharpton *(center)*, and Alton Maddox *(far right)*— led a march toward Mayor Ed Koch's residence at Gracie Mansion in New York City. The Brawley case divided the city and galvanized considerable opposition against Sharpton.

Frederick Scoralic was the longtime sheriff of Dutchess County, where Brawley lived. Three days after she was found, one of the men named as a possible attacker, Harry Crist, a part-time policeman from Fishkill, New York, killed himself.

SHARPTON'S INVOLVEMENT

For Sharpton, getting involved in the case was an easy decision, in one way. "I cannot describe the horror I felt upon hearing the full details of this story," he wrote. "No black person is without historical memory of the outrages visited upon black women throughout slavery and into the 20th century." In another way, the case complicated an already busy time in Sharpton's life. The Howard Beach verdict was delivered nine days after Brawley was found. Sharpton recalls the period by calling it "the most complex and trying time in my life."

Sharpton, Maddox, and Mason claimed that officials all the way up to the state government were trying to suppress the case to protect the white defendants. They specifically named Stephen Pagones, an assistant district attorney in Dutchess County, as both a racist and one of the rapists. At the height of the case's publicity, a poll conducted in the summer of 1988 showed 85 percent of whites thought Brawley was lying, while 51 percent of blacks thought her story was invented.

Abrams put together a grand jury to hear evidence. Even without speaking to Brawley, the jurors conducted 180 interviews, saw 250 exhibits, and reviewed 6,000 pages of testimony. The jury's final report was decisive: Brawley had invented her story and the accusations against Pagones were "false and had no basis in fact."

Medical evidence did not confirm Brawley's claim of sexual abuse. Despite her report of being held captive for four days, she appeared well nourished, not suffering from any winter exposure, and had appeared to brush her teeth recently. Other witnesses said the story was an invention of the teen to avoid punishment from her parents for staying out late repeatedly.

The fallout from the case was immediate. Maddox was suspended indefinitely from practicing law after he failed to attend a hearing questioning his conduct in the case. Pagones sued Maddox, Mason, and Sharpton for defamation of character. He was awarded $345,000 when the jury found Sharpton liable for making seven defamatory statements about the assistant district attorney. (Maddox was found

"If We Didn't Have an Al Sharpton, We'd Have to Invent One."

Years after the Brawley case, Sharpton explained how he got through such a tumultuous time with his beliefs intact. He said his tactics in the case, which included leading a march to support her, were learned from "top-notch civil rights strategists." He recalled:

It took until the early nineties before anyone white would admit I had a following, but one of the things that kept me going during the Brawley case was that I knew that a lot of black people were behind me, that I was saying what they wanted said. They may not have had the nerve to say it themselves—they had to be concerned for their jobs and families—but they wanted it said. The reason I knew this was that they would say it to me.

In a profile in the *New Yorker*, Sharpton went further in making this distinction. The author wrote, "Shaming as the whole episode might have been to some, Sharpton invoked it ... as an illustration of the high standing that whites can't, or simply won't, credit him with."

"No one ever stopped to say, 'Well, why would those guys do that,'" he said about his benefactors who paid his fine, including businessman Percy Sutton. "It's because in their own minds and their own hearts they feel I'm saying and doing things they know are right and can't do themselves. Percy Sutton used to have an expression, 'If we didn't have an Al Sharpton, we'd have to invent one.' ... What people have never stopped and thought about is that no one can survive as long as I have unless somebody needs them."

When asked about the Brawley incident by this author during an interview in early 2010, Sharpton might have shown a hint of contrition. He said it is not mentioned much anymore and people have accepted that he believed the teenager and that he will not apologize for believing her. "When Duke happened and I didn't go, people said, well he didn't go knee-jerk. It's surprising how many people on the right wing say Tawana Brawley and Duke. It's hard to stop somebody's career on one case when there haven't been other Brawleys."

Sharpton was referencing the case in 2006 when an African-American exotic dancer claimed that three white Duke University lacrosse players sexually assaulted her at a party. A month after the accusations were made—and after literally hundreds of stories were written—all charges against the players were dropped. Although the prosecutor for the case called the incident a "hate crime," Sharpton never got involved.

guilty of making two such statements and Mason one.) Sharpton refused to pay his share of the settlement, $65,000; a number of black business leaders later collected money to pay this debt.

NO APOLOGY

Almost as famous as the Brawley case itself is Sharpton's refusal to apologize for his actions. He has never said he agrees with the verdict or that he regretted his actions against Pagones. "I think people might like to explain my ferocious involvement as overemotional zeal, but the fact is, Tawana was never disproved," he wrote in his first book. "Can I say that I know beyond a shadow of a doubt what happened? No. Neither can my critics. We haven't proven anything definitely, but it hasn't been dismissed. . . . I believe Tawana, to this day. I have always believed her and always will. And I believe Robert Abrams lied on me. As a matter of fact, I know he did."

Not everyone, however, holds the same opinion. In a major Sharpton profile published in the *New York Times*, Adam Nagourney wrote:

> [Sharpton keeps] identifying himself with a case that made him at once indelibly famous and, in many circles, politically toxic. . . . The girl's tale of rape and abuse is one that no impartial judge or jury has ever accepted, but one that Sharpton, despite the strong urging of such self-described admirers as Edward I. Koch, former mayor of New York, has declined to renounce, to his lasting detriment.
>
> It was the kind of debacle that should have ended any hope Sharpton had of becoming a national political force and limited his audience to [a] few hundred people. . . . And it is why the mere mention of Sharpton's name draws, to this day, startlingly different reactions in different neighborhoods of New York: he is seen as inspirational or repellent; as the principled civil rights leader battling police brutality

and a hostile mayor or as the publicity-seeking huckster, willing to ride the misery of others to fame.

CRITICISM ON ALL SIDES

Sharpton gets criticism from Republicans and Democrats about the Brawley case. Many Republicans, such as Rush Limbaugh, find few topics on which they agree with Sharpton. Limbaugh, a national conservative radio host, has criticized Sharpton for years, blaming him for a variety of faults, including the Brawley case.

In 2009, years after the Brawley incident, when Limbaugh tried to buy an NFL team, Sharpton returned the criticism, writing a letter to the NFL commissioner opposing the move. Eventually, Limbaugh was not allowed to buy a football team, but not before he said this about Sharpton's letter on his radio show:

> Now, this saddens me as well. This disappoints me. I know Reverend Sharpton. Sharpton is better than this. He knows better than this. You know, I didn't judge Al Sharpton's fitness to be in radio when he wanted to earn an honest living, for once, given his well-documented past, [as] the author of the Tawana Brawley hoax. I believe in freedom, second chances, and I also don't discriminate.

On the other hand, Eric Altman, the author of a number of political books and a well-known blog for the liberal magazine the *Nation*, says of Sharpton's actions during the Brawley case: "The entire Tawana Brawley episode makes me sick, not least of which for the idealistic people [Sharpton] deliberately misled as well as the reputations of honest cops he sought to destroy."

"We are friends," said Koch, the mayor of New York during the Brawley case and a lifelong Democrat, in a 2003 interview with the Web site *The Left Coaster*, "but I have told [Sharpton] repeatedly that unless he repudiates the Tawana Brawley hoax he will never be a crossover leader that people can follow."

Sharpton has also had run-ins with journalists about the Brawley case. In 2007, NBC's political correspondent David Gregory had a famous confrontation with Sharpton when Gregory was guest the MSNBC show *Hardball.* Sharpton was on the show to talk about Don Imus, the radio talk show host who was then in trouble for criticizing the Rutgers University women's basketball team in a derogatory way. As Sharpton called for Imus to be fired, Gregory pressed him about the Brawley case, calling it more serious than Imus's slur about the basketball team. He criticized Sharpton for failing to apologize in that case, even though the court found him guilty of defamation of character.

5

Bensonhurst and
a Murder Attempt

Eight months after the Tawana Brawley case ended, Al Sharpton and Attorney General Robert Abrams were on the opposite sides of another case, only this one was a lot more personal for Sharpton. On June 29, 1989, the 34-year-old preacher was arrested and charged with stealing at least $250,000 from the organization that he had started more than 15 years earlier. The next day, Sharpton was arrested again, this time charged with tax evasion, in Albany, New York.

In the first set of charges, Sharpton faced 67 counts of grand larceny, as well as falsifying business records and scheming to defraud. Abrams said he took money from the group National Youth Movement, which Sharpton started in 1971. The charges stated that between 1985 and 1988, Sharpton improperly represented the group as a nonprofit when he solicited money from a number of Fortune 500 companies and individuals. In Albany, he was charged with income tax evasion as the state alleged that his group, the National Youth Movement, never filed any tax returns and did not

On June 29, 1989, Al Sharpton is led away in handcuffs from Manhattan Criminal Court after being arraigned on a 67-count indictment. He was accused of stealing money from the charitable group he had launched in New York.

fill out the paperwork necessary to be considered a nonprofit group.

Sharpton has probably been arrested more times than even he could count, but the vast majority of these arrests have been for disorderly conduct, charges that usually disappear without jail time. If he were found guilty of stealing money, however, he would face a five-year sentence. The income tax evasion charges carried a possible four-year sentence.

Despite the seriousness of the charges, Sharpton aggressively—but also playfully—attacked the charges. When word leaked to him that his arrest was imminent, he told a reporter that he would join the "black leader tax indictment Hall of Fame," citing Martin Luther King Jr., Adam Clayton Powell Jr., and Marcus Garvey as other leaders who were arrested on the same charges.

When the day came and Sharpton was asked in court how he pleaded, he quipped, "I plead the Attorney General insane." When officers went to lead a handcuffed Sharpton outside in front of a throng of people, he shouted, "They did this to King! They did this to Powell! They did this to Garvey! This is my inauguration! I have arrived!" The police told him to be quiet, but he refused. When they went to put him in the car, he popped back up and said, "He's messing up my hair," getting laughs.

In his autobiography, Sharpton said he did this not to mock the legal system and be a clown but to send a message to Abrams that he was not getting him and to let the black community know he was all right. The plan worked: The next day's headlines in the New York *Daily News* read, "67 Counts— Sharpton Pleads Att. General Insane."

The trial started almost immediately. Everything about the trial was big, including the size of the jury pool (second only to the one for organized crime mob boss John Gotti, he was told) and the size of the courtroom, which held 300 people. He recalled in *Go and Tell Pharaoh*: "I told the press, being provocative in a way that I now regret, 'If y'all are gonna lynch me, you're going to have to get the biggest tree, no small tree will do, 'cause I'm a big n-----.'"

The four-month trial had 83 witnesses. Bank records showed that most of Sharpton's transactions took place in cash, including paying employees. When the prosecution was finished, his attorney, Alton Maddox Jr., told Sharpton, "I'm going to do something very risky. I want you to trust me. I'm going to rest, I'm not going to call any witnesses. They've put on a very weak case, they haven't proven anything, so why let them tear at our defense?" Sharpton said he was nervous, but he agreed, in part because he was exhausted from the trial and the other civil rights cases he had been involved in. The strategy shocked everyone.

When the verdict came back, he was found not guilty for each of the 67 counts of stealing money. He then went upstate to face the tax-evasion charges. When the court there decided he could not be tried, he was home free. The court reasoned if Sharpton had not stolen the money as charged, then he could not have evaded taxes on it. A notoriously bad record keeper, Sharpton did, however, get fined for not paying state income taxes one year but served no jail time.

BENSONHURST

With the publicity from Brawley and his tax trial, Sharpton was in the media frequently, increasing the number of cases where people tried to secure his help. While it sometimes could be difficult to decide which cases to help out with, the preacher's next big case was easy to pick.

As with the Howard Beach incident, the case in Bensonhurst started with a simple misunderstanding. Soon, however, racial tensions sparked violence, and the protests that followed quickly turned this event into another one that became known simply by the name of the neighborhood where it occurred. Bensonhurst is in the southwestern part of Brooklyn and comprised of many Italian families.

On August 23, 1989, Yusef Hawkins, a 16-year-old African-American boy, and three friends, went to Brooklyn to investigate buying a used car they saw advertised for $900. The four got off the subway at the wrong stop and ran into a group of Italian-American kids, who were lying in wait because they were supposedly upset to learn that a neighborhood girl (also Italian American) was dating a black man. The crowd chased the four and Hawkins ended up dead, shot twice in the heart. Police found seven baseball bats and four spent .32-caliber bullet casings at the scene of the crime.

Sharpton was involved immediately, starting marches similar to the one he conducted in Howard Beach to help keep the plight of the slain boy in the news and try to ensure the killers were brought to justice. "This march made Howard Beach look like summer camp," Sharpton wrote in his first autobiography. "Thousands of whites were lining the sidewalks, yelling obscenities and holding up watermelons. As the marchers chanted, 'We want the killer,' a woman yelled back, 'We want to kill you.'"

Five people were arrested in the case, two of whom were charged with murder. A key witness in the case disappeared and refused to testify when he was found. Joseph Fama, the 19-year-old who shot Hawkins, was found guilty of second-degree murder and received a sentence of 32 and a half years. The leader of the group, Keith Mondello, 19 at the time, was acquitted of murder and manslaughter charges but was found guilty of 12 lesser charges. He received a sentence of 5 to 16 years in jail.

STABBING

The Bensonhurst case demonstrated the power Sharpton had accrued by that point. He called march after march to keep up publicity in the case, to argue for longer sentences for those found guilty, and to pressure prosecutors to convict more members who were part of the mob. On the afternoon of January 12, 1991, Sharpton readied for his twenty-ninth march for the case. Despite the number, Sharpton was able to draw good crowds of protesters each time, with about 200 people for this march that was starting at Public School 205.

This time, however, would be different. Ever since the Brawley case, Sharpton knew the danger in the opposition he attracted. While his wife, Kathy, and two daughters, Dominique and Ashley, often marched with him, he made sure they were not right next to him, both to protect them from possible violence and to keep their pictures out of the newspapers.

As he was preparing for this march, he remembers, "Suddenly, I felt someone punch me in the chest." A white man flashed past him and Sharpton said, "He had this contorted look of hatred on his face. . . . Before I could get a clear look at him, I looked down and saw a knife sticking out of my chest. 'Oh my God, he stabbed me.'" Sharpton pulled the knife out, felt the pain, and slumped to the ground with blood all over his hands.

The assailant tried to flee, but was stopped by protesters, including Hawkins's brother, who knocked him down. The crowd started to beat the man, 27-year-old Michael Riccardi, but police intervened and arrested him. Riccardi, who police said was drunk, had plunged a five-inch (12.7 centimeter) steak knife into Sharpton's upper left chest, narrowly missing his lung and any major blood vessels.

At the hospital, Sharpton, who was dressed in his typical attire that day—a jogging suit and a full-length leather coat his wife had bought him—made the emergency personnel stop cutting his clothes off so he could remove the coat without harming it. Blood was drained from his chest cavity and doctors told him he would stay in the hospital for three to four days. He was listed in serious, but stable, condition.

Even this incident carried some controversy with it. When Mayor David Dinkins of New York visited Sharpton in the hospital that night, he came out and told the media that the preacher had called for peace. Sharpton's lawyer, Alton Maddox, disagreed, saying, "The only one speaking for Reverend Sharpton is Alton Maddox and I'm not calling for peace."

Once he stabilized, Sharpton immediately called his longtime friend, the Reverend Jesse Jackson. Throughout the years, the two men have had an up-and-down relationship, but the next day Jackson was at Sharpton's bedside, jokingly telling him the only reason he was not seriously hurt was because Sharpton "had seven inches [17.7 cm] of fat and they used a six-inch [15.2 cm] knife." The photo of the two Baptist rever-

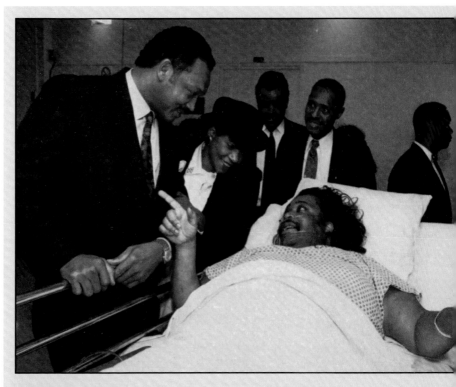

On January 13, 1991, Al Sharpton talks to Jesse Jackson *(left)* from his hospital bed in New York, where he was recuperating from a knife wound received in an attack the day before. Also visiting Sharpton are *(from left)* singer Melba Moore, union leader Jim Bell, and the Reverend Herber Daughtry.

ends together was played prominently in the *New York Times* the next day. During Sharpton's short hospital stay, Cardinal John O'Connor, archbishop of the Roman Catholic Archdiocese of New York, wrote about Sharpton's nonviolent ways, radio shock jock Howard Stern visited him, and the entire fifth-grade class at P.S. 205, where the stabbing took place, sent him a homemade get-well card.

Although the wound was not life-threatening, it did take Sharpton two months to fully recover. During that time, he and his family went to Las Vegas, where Jackson and his family joined them. Sharpton said the incident changed his life in one way, making him question how he tried to achieve some of his goals. He decided to try to avoid unnecessary public fights and concentrate more on what he called "real Christian work."

Al Sharpton and Jesse Jackson

At first glance, it appears that almost everything Sharpton has tried to accomplish, the Reverend Jesse Jackson did first. Jackson, who is 13 years older than Sharpton, was a Baptist preacher, worked in the civil rights movement alongside the Reverend Martin Luther King Jr., and mounted a serious campaign for president, all before Sharpton did some of the same tasks.

While Sharpton admits he learned much from Jackson, their relationship has veered from friendship to accusations back to friendship. He explains:

> A relationship between a 26-, 27-year-old man and a 13-year-old kid changes when the kid is 30 and you're 43. [It changes] even more when the kid is 45 and you're 60. It goes from being cute to being a rival, it was a natural thing we had to work through.
>
> The difference between James Brown and Jesse Jackson was that Jesse and I were in the same field. James Brown was never threatened by me. James Brown had the same relationship with Michael Jackson that I have with Jesse Jackson.... [When an incident happens], you have to wonder who the *Today* show is going to call.

In an interview with *Salon*, Sharpton expanded on the differences between his relationship with Jackson and the one he had with Brown. "I'd say James Brown was my father, Jesse Jackson was my teacher. Jesse helped me with political and ministerial issues. James Brown was more personal. I would talk to James Brown about a girlfriend, or what clothes to buy."

Often it has seemed that Sharpton has tried to elbow Jackson out of the way, starting in 2001 when it was revealed that Jackson had fathered a child out of wedlock. The revelation diminished Jackson's standing, and Sharpton seemed only too happy to fill the void.

The major rift, however, according to Sharpton, was the close work Jackson did with President Bill Clinton. "I felt Jesse used his tremendous access

CROWN HEIGHTS

In both Howard Beach and Bensonhurst, the cases pitted Italian Americans against African Americans. After an incident on August 19, 1991, Sharpton found himself fighting another prominent group of New Yorkers, the Hasidim—a branch of

to the White House to help Sandy Weill [head of the large bank Citigroup] and those Wall Street guys more than to help working people and consumers. He got too close to power. Our conflict is also generational. There is a younger voter that Jesse can't reach that I can. . . . Jesse doesn't have the defiance that I have."

In the same article, published in 2001 in *New York* magazine, Jackson refused several times to criticize or even comment on the record about his relationship with Sharpton: "It's cultural racism to reduce black life to a story about me and Al. . . . This is sick."

One of the few times Sharpton has publicly admitted he was wrong involves a criticism he made of Jackson. While being interviewed from jail one time, Sharpton repeated the sometimes-told but inaccurate story about Jackson smearing the blood of Martin Luther King Jr. on his shirt to declare himself the "blood successor" to the great civil rights leader. While Jackson was with King when he was shot, no one at the scene ever charged Jackson with doing that. Sharpton had blundered and he issued a "sincere and unconditional" apology to his mentor, saying in a letter to Jackson, "I do not now, and have never believed, you acted improperly at the scene of King's assassination."

In 2005, Sharpton made this confession to a reporter from *New York*. He said he had recently apologized to Jackson for the way he had treated him in the press:

> I realized that personal ambition had a lot to do with motivating my disagreements with him. Somewhere along the way, the student gets the misconception that your rise is dependent on the moving on of the teacher, and it has nothing to do with that. He'd invested a lot in me, and believed in me before anyone thought I'd be viable, and it was wrong for me to feel that my ambition was more important than our relationship.

Orthodox Judaism founded in eighteenth-century Eastern Europe. On the night of the incident, the motorcade of the grand rabbi of the Lubavitcher, a Hasidic Jewish sect, ran a red light as it sped through the Crown Heights section of Brooklyn. The motorcade had the permission of the police to run the light; in fact, it had a police escort at the time. When the car swerved to avoid another car, it hit two black children, seven-year-old Gavin Cato and his cousin Angela.

When the driver, Yusef Lifsh, got out of the car to check on the children's condition and try to get them out from under the car, angry bystanders started to beat him. Lifsh was taken away in a private ambulance before the two children were brought to the hospital. Cato was killed and his cousin was badly injured.

Riots followed, as a crowd of approximately 250 African Americans moved toward Kingston Avenue, a predominantly Jewish section of the neighborhood. Cars were vandalized, rocks were thrown, and a group of 20 young black men eventually surrounded Yankel Rosenbaum, a 29-year-old student. Rosenbaum was stabbed several times and beaten, and he died later that night. Riots continued for three days, with Jews beaten, stores looted, and houses and cars vandalized. Even the police commissioner's car was overturned in melees that followed.

Some said that Sharpton incited more violence with the statements he made at Cato's funeral. During his eulogy, according to an article on the Slate Web site, Sharpton said:

> The world will tell us he was killed by accident. Yes, it was a social accident.... It's an accident to allow an apartheid ambulance service in the middle of Crown Heights.... Talk about how Oppenheimer in South Africa sends diamonds straight to Tel Aviv and deals with the diamond merchants right here in Crown Heights. The issue is not anti-Semitism; the issue is apartheid.... All we want to say is what Jesus

On August 26, 1991, Al Sharpton *(fourth from left)* walks in a funeral procession for seven-year-old Gavin Cato, who was killed in a car accident in the Crown Heights neighborhood of Brooklyn, New York. Cato's death sparked riots, looting, and anti-Semitic violence in Crown Heights. Walking with Sharpton are *(from left)* Robert "Sonny" Carson, the Reverend Herbert Daughtry, and Carmel Cato, Gavin's father.

said: If you offend one of these little ones, you got to pay for it. No compromise, no meetings, no kaffe klatsch, no skinnin' and grinnin.' Pay for your deeds.

When a grand jury declined to indict Yusef Lifsh, the car's driver, he was whisked out of the country to Israel. When Sharpton and others brought a civil suit against him for the hospital costs and funeral bills, Lifsh could not be notified about the possible lawsuit because he was out of the country.

Sharpton boarded the official Israeli airline to go to Tel Aviv and serve Lifsh with the lawsuit papers. Everybody on the plane knew why he was going to Tel Aviv, and with the vast majority of passengers being Jewish, tension was high. When a woman yelled at him, "Go to hell, Sharpton," he responded, "I am in hell." The next day, tabloid newspapers ran the headline "Sharpton says Israel is Hell."

Life did not get any easier once Sharpton's plane landed in Israel. Numerous cab drivers refused to drive him, until finally he found an Arab driver who would take him to the American Embassy. Unable to find Lifsh, he left the country without serving him.

6

Political Aspirations

Given the vehement feelings about Al Sharpton, both pro and con, after seven years of almost constant turns in the spotlight, the last thing people expected was for him to run for public office. Yet that is exactly what Sharpton did. He did not choose to run for a position in the state government in New York or even an empty district seat that would make him a U.S. congressman. He chose instead to run for the United States Senate in one of the most hotly contested races in New York history.

The deck was stacked against him from the beginning. Before even considering his opponents, the Brawley case had been less than four years earlier, and he was still under indictment for tax fraud.

In a state that typically votes for Democrats, Sharpton became the fourth candidate on the Democratic side in the 1992 race. He was by far the least experienced. All the Democrats were vying for the opportunity to oppose the incumbent Republican senator, Alphonse D'Amato. Fighting with Sharpton was front-runner Congresswoman Geraldine Ferraro; New York City Comptroller Elizabeth Holtzman, and New York State Attorney General Robert Abrams. There was, of course, no love lost between Abrams and Sharpton, who had fought close battles in the Brawley case and the preacher's tax evasion case. In his autobiography, Sharpton laid out what was at stake for him in this race:

> In many ways I risked my career to do so, because the media had painted me as a loudmouth, a walking sound bite, a con artist, a charlatan, and, worst of all, an imposter, with no real constituency and no true issues, a self-created media manipulator. One critic went so far as to call me "a practitioner of the big lie." What hurt most in all this—and feels patronizing—was that my vilifiers and critics never tried to look at me as a man and as a person. How could they know what I was talking about if they didn't know where I'd been? How could they know if the conditions I was complaining about and demanding redress for were actual if they didn't come look? I was speaking for people who didn't normally have a voice, I was speaking from neighborhoods that didn't normally gain attention. I had to be dramatic, I had to be loud.

He had to work just to get on the ballot. He campaigned as he had lived, saying dramatic things such as that he had "the right to throw my hair into the ring," or that he was the first person in the nation to run against two people who had arrested him. (Both Holtzman and Abrams had initiated legal cases against Sharpton.)

In a tough campaign, he did not go negative. He said he had an agenda. He wanted a special prosecutor to be permanently appointed; he was against tax breaks for corporations; and he said he wanted to talk about Haiti and its peoples' fight for

On September 10, 1992, four Democratic hopefuls for the U.S. Senate gather on the WABC-TV set in New York City during their televised debate. From left the candidates are Al Sharpton, Robert Abrams, Liz Holtzman, and Geraldine Ferraro.

democracy. He borrowed a technique from Jackson and stayed in people's houses as he traveled. "The campaign became like a crusade," he wrote.

Sharpton spent just $63,000—a miniscule amount compared with his opponents. Polls estimated he would get 5 percent of the vote. When the votes were totaled, however, Sharpton had been underestimated again—what was shaping up to be a constant theme in his life. He ended up garnering 16 percent of the vote, or 166,000 votes. He earned two out of every three African-American votes cast statewide. He did not finish fourth either; in fact, he beat Holtzman. Abrams won the primary but later lost a close race to D'Amato.

BUILDING ON THE BASE

Jumping into 1992's race was a daring venture where Sharpton tested his popularity in a new arena. Having gone much further than he could have imagined, he aimed much higher two years later. The 1992 race had pitted Sharpton against a strong field of competitors, but none of the other three Democrats were incumbents. In 1994, Sharpton again decided to run for the other of New York's two U.S. Senate seats, but this time he took on an iconic Democrat, Daniel Patrick Moynihan.

Moynihan was a three-term senator running for reelection. Typically, incumbents do not face primaries in their own parties, but instead wait for the other party to pick a challenger. As daunting as that was—and some would call it another race that Sharpton had no hope of winning—Moynihan was more than just a senator of 18 years; he had also worked in the four presidential administrations prior to his first election, starting as assistant secretary of labor for President John F. Kennedy. A revered liberal, Moynihan was also an academic, having worked as a sociologist for Harvard University and the Massachusetts Institute of Technology.

Sharpton remembered his second political effort fondly in *Go and Tell Pharaoh*:

> By 1994 I had reached, in my personal development, a place of deepening maturity and responsibility that had been building since the stabbing. I had to go from being the critic of society to actively trying to do something about it.... I wanted to be more than articulate, I want to create change.

For the most part, Moynihan did not engage Sharpton at all, refusing to debate him. Again, Sharpton ran on the cheap, spending just $100,000. In 1992, he got 166,000 votes out of the 1.2 million votes cast. This time, with only two candidates running, he did even better, drawing 187,000 votes out of the 700,000 cast.

Sharpton then ran for mayor three years later, in 1997, fighting his closest primary race ever with Manhattan Borough President Ruth Messinger. New York City campaign rules state that a candidate in a primary needs to gain at least 40 percent of the vote to win, no matter how many people are running. With Sharpton running an aggressive campaign, he garnered 32 percent of the Democratic vote in a primary on September 9. Messinger outpointed him, but was teetering on the 40 percent mark. A runoff election between the two candidates was set, but ultimately canceled when the Board of Elections's final count put Messinger just above 40 percent. Messinger was defeated soundly in the general election by incumbent Rudolph Giuliani, a Republican who won his second term as mayor.

RACE FOR THE WHITE HOUSE

With his political reputation growing, Sharpton's next try for public office sought to bring him all the way to 1600 Pennsylvania Avenue. On January 5, 2003, he joined the crowded race for the 2004 Democratic nomination for the White House. Ten people eventually entered the presidential race for the right to oppose the incumbent, George W. Bush, including five senators or former senators, one former governor, one retired U.S. general, two United States representatives, and the Reverend Al Sharpton.

In some instances, Sharpton took the race very seriously, although from the beginning he never had a real chance to win. He published a second autobiography, *Al on America*, coauthored with Karen Hunter. Although this book came out in 2002, it was obviously completed with an eye toward national office. The book included Sharpton's views on the Middle East, Cuba, Africa, and Vieques. He stated his support for gay marriage emphatically, saying it was an insult to be

On July 28, 2004, Al Sharpton spoke at the 2004 Democratic National Convention in Boston, Massachusetts. Sharpton had been one of 10 Democratic candidates who entered the presidential race that year; the nomination ultimately went to Senator John Kerry of Massachusetts.

asked about the topic. "It's like asking do I support black marriage or white marriage," he said. "The inference of the question is that gays are not like other human beings." Sharpton also spoke out against cruelty to animals, making a video for People for the Ethical Treatment of Animals (PETA).

The introduction to his book plainly stated his goals:

It's time for a leader who understands that our greatest strength is our differences. And being united—not just presenting a united front—is our greatest weapon. The next leader for this country must be able to look at all America

and see her for what she will become and then work tirelessly to see her become it. I am that leader.

One of the lesser-known facts about Sharpton is his dis-
dain for some Democrats. While most politicians and public
figures are friendlier to people perceived to be on the "same
side" as they are, Sharpton would openly criticize Democrats
if he disagreed with their actions or their opinions. When he
announced his candidacy, he wrote:

> I am running to take out the DLC, which I call the Demo-
> cratic Leisure Class, because that's who it serves—the leisure
> class and the wealthy. They are pro-deregulation of busi-
> ness. They are openly anti affirmative-action and pro-death
> penalty. In many ways they are no different from the Repub-
> licans. I see them as elephants in donkey's clothes.

So why would Sharpton go through the effort of running
if he knew he had little chance to upset the party favorites,
such as Senator John Kerry, Senator John Edwards, or former
governor Howard Dean? When his friend and mentor Jesse
Jackson mounted the first serious run for the White House by
an African American in 1984, he won five primaries and 21
percent of the vote, before losing to eventual nominee Walter
Mondale. In 1988, Jackson was an even stronger candidate,
winning 11 contests and 6.9 million votes. His second time
around Jackson was able to influence the Democratic agenda
put forward by eventual nominee Michael Dukakis.

The *New York Times* took its guess about Sharpton's reasons
for running in the headline of a story about his candidacy,
"Sharpton Runs for Presidency, and Influence." A former aide
was even clearer when he told the paper, "I think Al is posi-
tioning himself to be leader of black America."

When he faced repeated questions about trying usurp power
from Jackson, Sharpton answered them in a speech given to

the NAACP: "They make an issue this week on whether or not Reverend Jackson or Reverend Sharpton is going to dominate. I'm not running against Reverend Jackson." He added, "But can we only listen to one Negro at a time?"

Even friends wondered about his motives. An old friend, David McKee, a civil rights organizer from Chicago, told the *New York Times*, "On one hand, he has an intolerance of injus-

IN HIS OWN WORDS

The following is an excerpt from Al Sharpton's address to the Democratic National Convention in 2004:

Forty years ago, in 1964, Fannie Lou Hamer and the Mississippi Freedom Democratic Party stood at the Democratic convention in Atlantic City fighting to preserve voting rights for all Americans and all Democrats, regardless of race or gender. Hamer's stand inspired Dr. King's march in Selma, which brought about the Voting Rights Act of 1965.

Twenty years ago, Reverend Jesse Jackson stood at the Democratic National Convention in San Francisco, again, appealing to preserve those freedoms. Tonight, we stand with those freedoms at risk and our security as citizens in question....

The promise of America says we will guarantee quality education for all children and not spend more money on metal detectors than computers in our schools.... The promise of America provides that those who work in our health care system can afford to be hospitalized in the very beds they clean up every day. The promise of America is that government does not seek to regulate your behavior in the bedroom, but to guarantee your right to provide food in the kitchen....

[My mother taught me] that life is not where you start, but where you're going. That's family values.

I wanted somebody in my community to show that example. As I ran for president, I hoped that one child would come out of the ghetto like I did, could look at me walk across the stage with governors and senators and know they didn't have to be a drug dealer, they didn't have to be a hoodlum, they didn't have to be a gangster, they could stand up from a broken home, on welfare, and they could run for president of the United States.

tice. On the other hand, he is after a sense of recognition, a need for recognition." In the article, the reporter pointed out that during the heat of the campaign, Sharpton did choose to stay off the road for a week while he practiced to host *Saturday Night Live.*

Some members of the leadership in the Democratic Party were so worried Sharpton would monopolize the black vote and gain power with a good showing that they drafted Carol Moseley Braun, the first female African-American senator, to enter the race, hoping she would draw support from Sharpton.

They need not have feared. Lacking the widespread appeal, campaign money, and organizational team needed to mount a nationwide race, Sharpton never found his footing in the race. As a result, he did not surpass expectations, failing to win a single state primary or caucus. Although he was the second-to-last candidate to leave the race (Representative Dennis Kucinich was the last), he secured only 27 convention delegates to the eventual Democratic nominee's—John Kerry's—2,162.

Sharpton's lack of record keeping continued to plague him when he was forced to repay $100,000 in public funds he received because he exceeded federal limits on personal expenditures for the campaign. His last campaign finance filing showed that his campaign ended with a debt near $500,000. In 2009, five years after the race, the Federal Elections Commission fined Sharpton $285,000 for breaking campaign finance rules during his presidential campaign.

In 2010, when Sharpton looked back on the race—and in particular, the jockeying that occurred between himself and Moseley Braun—he mused that even though some people tried to stop him, he ended up accomplishing his main goal in the election, which was to become the de facto leader of the civil rights movement in the country.

7

Working With, and Against, the Media

The Reverend Al Sharpton naturally seems to split groups into pro and con, with strong feelings on both sides. No one, however, doubts his ability to make use of the media to suit his interests and needs. Everyone seems to agree that Sharpton has mastered the fast-paced world of TV interviews by making provocative statements and attending attention-getting events. So it may be a surprise to hear that Sharpton found this effort not natural, but a chore. He notes:

> [People say,] Oh Sharpton's always on the media, like that's an easy job. These reporters are there to cut my head off, they're not there to try to help me. When I'm on Bill O'Reilly [the conservative host of *The O'Reilly Factor* on Fox News Channel], they're there to take their best shot. I always tell people, if you think it's easy, step right up.... Given this technology [if I say something wrong], it'll be on all the

time. I've got to watch what I say three hours a day on radio.
I'm constantly under scrutiny.

Being available at the drop of a hat disrupts his schedule
constantly, but Sharpton frequently answers the call when TV
stations want an opinion on the topic of the day. As he showed
during his previously mentioned trip to NBC, his familiarity
with the procedure does allow him to streamline the time and
effort required for every visit. At NBC, for the second time
that morning, he was ushered quickly through security with
the help of a staffer. He bantered easily with the staff in the
makeup room, knowing exactly what little touchups he needed
before going in front of the camera. Once in the studio, he
waited less than 10 minutes to be on the air, and then handled
the interview quickly. Down the hall he went, out the door to
his waiting car and driver.

Sharpton, of course, has worked tirelessly to achieve this
recognition and to have his opinion valued, whether the stories are related to civil rights or not. Being easily recognized
on the street may be good for one's ego, but it does carry a
price, erasing some of his privacy and making him reconsider
his security.

After his first few big national cases, Sharpton began to
realize the changes that were occurring. "I became conscious
of the price that I was going to have to pay," he wrote, looking
back on his life since 1986.

> In the years since, I have faced tax trials, I've had 15 or 16
> different arrests and jailings [by 2010, he would be have
> more than 20 arrests], I've spent as much as 30 days in jail at
> one time for demonstrations. Once I had six different trials
> going at the same time. [During] Days of Outrage, I stopped
> the BQE [the Brooklyn-Queens Expressway, a major high-
> way connecting Brooklyn to Queens], I closed the Statue of
> Liberty. I don't think people see the downside of all this. I've

spent as much time in courts and jails as I have anywhere else in the last 10 years.

That's how my life has changed. This is not fun. I can't do the things that normal people do without seriously considering what I'm doing. What I have realized is that I will always be Al Sharpton. I can't get up tomorrow morning like the average person and say, "OK, I've done that, now I'm going to try something else." I will be Al Sharpton until the day I die. The door back to normal life is closed for me now. I know that. I think I've given my identity up to the cause. . . . So, yes, I'm known, my name's out there, but what it really means is that I spend a lot of nights in hotels by myself, because nothing—going for a walk, getting something to eat, meeting friends for coffee—is simple anymore. Life has changed.

TAKING PLENTY OF MEDIA CRITICISM

For someone who is considered a friend of the media, always ready to answer a question or give a quote, Sharpton has taken some of the harshest criticism in memory from a variety of sources.

An editor of a weekly black newspaper portrayed why whites have so much contempt for Sharpton: "He's fat; he has show-business hair, a gold medal, a jumpsuit, and Reeboks. He's a perfect stereotype of a pork-chop preacher." A 1988 story in the *New York Times* that examined Sharpton's influence was headlined "Sharpton: Champion or Opportunist?" The piece states that supporters view him "as an authentic, stirring leader who has challenged the city and state power structure too often to be doubted; who is not afraid to march in white neighborhoods or to tell blacks, as he did recently, that 'we can turn this city on or off when we get ready.'"

The story goes on to give the opposition viewpoint:

To others, the minister from Brooklyn is a fringe figure in the equal rights causes he espouses—a publicity-hungry creature of television whose rhetoric and flamboyance mask limited achievements, a self-aggrandizer whose early promise as a youth leader has been lost in the free-wheeling worlds of music and boxing, where his connections are indisputable.

A 2002 *New Yorker* profile contained this scathing bit of criticism:

> When I told Michael Meyers, the director of the New York Civil Rights Coalition, that I was writing about Sharpton, he blew up at me. "Al Sharpton is a media hound," he said. "He's a racial buffoon, a publicity stunt, and you guys fall in line. I want to know what has he ever done for quote-unquote his people, whoever they are?" Meyers, who is also a columnist for the *New York Post* and is black, went on to argue that the media's coverage of Sharpton represented, in itself, a form of bias. "The credibility he had has been given by the New York Paternalistic Times," he said. "It's racism. It's sheer lunacy, but it's also racism."

That same story reminded readers that Ed Koch, who went on to become friends with Sharpton, once dubbed him "Al Charlatan." The story continued: "He has been variously condemned as a hustler, a demagogue, a symbol of all that is wrong with race relations in America, and a stupid joke."

Sharpton, as expected, answered in kind for all the criticism. To make his point, he reaches back to a little-known case. In 1989, Richard Earl Luke died in the custody of the housing police in the Queensbridge project where he lived. The next day, Sharpton was in the family's apartment, leading a prayer.

> I've regularly been called an outside agitator, but I have never taken a case, from Howard Beach to Brawley to Bensonhurst to Pannell or anything else, ... where the victims

Saturday Night Live

There are probably a lot of reasons politicians usually do not host *Saturday Night Live*: the irreverent humor, the possibility of embarrassing themselves live on national television, and the time it takes away from their first priority, governing. Equal time usually is not a consideration.

When the famous sketch comedy show asked the Reverend Al Sharpton to host in December 2003, however, he was then involved in a race to be president of the United States. Over the objections of most of his advisers, Sharpton agreed to host the show. When the show's creator, Lorne Michaels, was asked why he picked Sharpton, he said, "People are responding to him. Whether his candidacy is serious or not, he is being talked about."

Sharpton retained the right to veto any skits he was not comfortable with, and he did nix a skit that would have mocked Jesse Jackson. The reviews of his performance were mixed, but Sharpton won over most people in his opening monologue when he showed an ability to laugh at himself.

Sharpton opened the show is a dark suit, telling viewers he hoped they got to know the "real" him. Then actor Tracy Morgan appeared next to Sharpton, dressed in a caricature of "old" Sharpton, wearing a purple jogging suit, gold chains, a much bigger stomach and a much more flamboyant head of coiffed hair. After the two traded quips, with Sharpton finally admitting that, yes he did used to dress like that, the Morgan character said, "Look 'atcha. Up here, on this racist television show! All dressed up like Pat Boone. Trying to appeal to people in Iowa! You used to be the touring manager for James Brown, the Godfather of Soul!"

When the band started playing a James Brown song, the two began trading verses of "I Got You (I Feel Good)." The real Al Sharpton started an imitation of his own, doing a little James Brown–inspired dance.

"No one, including Lorne Michaels, knew I was going to do the James Brown," Sharpton said. "Just instinctively, I decided to add that dance, but after that I was convinced in my soul that I'd done the right thing."

Alas, because of campaign rules that demand equal time access for all candidates, 32 cities located where presidential primaries were coming up decided not to show the live Sharpton broadcast, instead running old *Saturday Night Live* reruns.

Al Sharpton pokes fun at himself on the December 6, 2003, episode of the NBC sketch comedy show *Saturday Night Live*. Pictured here with Sharpton is comedian Tracy Morgan, who plays a younger Al Sharpton.

... didn't call and ask me to help them. I only become involved if I am invited. Patricia Garcia, Richard Luke's mother, said something to me that touched me more than almost anything anyone else has said to me: "I wanted the whole world to know what they did to my son, and I knew of nothing else but you to get that done."

GAINING ACCEPTANCE

As Sharpton had hoped, his good showings in various political elections helped boost his media profile. After his first run for Senate, major profiles of him ran in the *New York Times* and the *New Yorker*. Connie Chung from CBS's *Eye to Eye* and Mike Wallace from *60 Minutes* both interviewed him for their programs.

A story in the *New York Times* in 2001, headlined "The Post-Sharpton Sharpton," showed how pleased he was with his new-found respect. Early in President George W. Bush's first term, Sharpton was in Congress to protest some recommendations made by the new administration. Suddenly, Sharpton found himself face-to-face with Secretary of State-designate Colin Powell. The former head of the Joint Chiefs of Staff, Powell was one of the most well-known and well-regarded African Americans in the country. Powell had taken a vastly different route than Sharpton to fame. Yet here they were, face-to-face thanks to a chance meeting.

Journalist Adam Nagourney captured the short but telling encounter:

> "Reverend Sharpton—how are you?" Powell said, grasping Sharpton's hand.
>
> "Congratulations, general: you did well," Sharpton responded.
>
> "We're going to do well," Powell responded, abandoning any pretense of small talk. "I think it's going to be an administration for all the people—and we'll convince you of that."
>
> Sharpton arched an eyebrow. "We'll see," he said.
>
> "We will see," Powell said, smiling politely. "This is my wife Alma."
>
> Powell and his entourage glided up the hall, but Sharpton stopped to consider his moment. Gen. Colin Powell treating Al Sharpton like a peer in the halls of the nation's Capitol.... Sharpton turned to the photographers in the hallway and said, "I think you just got your shot."

This level of popularity led to other offers, most of which the preacher says he turned down. One he did not refuse was the chance to host an eight-week reality show on Spike TV called *I Hate My Job*. Sharpton's role was to guide eight men through career makeovers. He talked about this decision in a 2005 profile in *New York* magazine in a story written by Erik Hedegaard:

> One of the things that drives me to do this kind of thing is, more young people are influenced by Comedy Central than by *60 Minutes*, so if you understand that, you understand why Al Sharpton would do a reality show.... Also, I happen to agree with the concept of people looking to discover what they're really on the planet for, because I had to go through that. And it gives you an eight-week series—and I don't know many people who'd turn down an eight-week series on TV!...
>
> I don't think that everyone who stops me on the street or in airports necessarily agrees with my politics.... What I think *SNL* in particular did, it showed that I do more than just get angry and protest. The right wing would love to project me as a hater and all of that. But I think America that night said, "This guy ain't no hater!" That show got the highest ratings of their season, so it put a human face on me in front of a maximum amount of American people, and now I have people of all races coming up to me.

While Sharpton has worked to become known as a leader of black Americans, various people have suggested that this title holds a lot less importance now than it did in the era of Martin Luther King Jr., or even when Jesse Jackson was running for president. With the election of Barack Obama as president of the United States in 2008, the figurative title may come to mean even less.

"There is not a civil rights movement anymore," H. Carl McCall, the state comptroller of New York, remarked in a story in the *New York Times*. "The civil rights movement has changed. I think the issue now for the African-American community is political empowerment, economic empowerment. In a sense, the civil rights era has migrated to those new major issues."

This 2001 story goes on to note, "There are moments when Sharpton seems like a Japanese soldier stranded on a Pacific island, still fighting World War II. His signature issue is battling police abuse, and white and black politicians praise his advances in that area."

8

Humanitarian Aid

Al Sharpton's fame, and opponents, were mostly forged through high-pressure cases that started with a terrible act of violence against an individual or small group of people. Sharpton is probably a preacher first and a civil rights activist second, but since the mid-1990s, he has added one more title to this list: humanitarian.

During his 1994 race against Daniel Patrick Moynihan, Sharpton took a six-day trip to Rwanda and the refugee camps in Zaire, Africa. This area of the country was in the midst of one of the worst genocides in the past 50 years. (Genocide is the systematic destruction of a group of people because of their race, religion, or another attribute. The most famous case of genocide is actually the event where the term was created, the Nazi campaign to destroy European Jews before and during World War II.)

The Rwanda genocide took place over a relatively short amount of time, about four months, but an estimated 800,000 people were killed. Most of the victims were Tutsi, and their deaths were a result of long-standing ethnic tension with another group, the Hutus. On his visit, Sharpton saw the terrible suffering, with children dying from lack of food and supplies. He saw orphan camps with 3,000 or more children; one camp called Goma had just eight doctors for 300,000 people. Yet the people Sharpton met remained proud and challenged America to assert its power and tell the world the truth of what was happening.

Sharpton believed trade with many African nations would help with the continent's very real domestic problems of poverty, famine, disease, and ceaseless war and genocide. "I think that we need to open Africa up to real trade. I think that we need to support democratic governments there with real trade. And we need to stop holding up, with our businesses, a lot of the archaic and the, in my judgment, murderous regimes that have dominated parts of Africa," he said on *Hardball,* an MSNBC show hosted by Chris Matthews.

HURRICANE KATRINA

In August 2005, one of the country's most devastating natural disasters happened when Hurricane Katrina ripped into the Gulf Coast. Nearly 2,000 people died after the levees failed around New Orleans, and 90 percent of Mississippi's beachfront towns were flooded with water reaching up to 12 miles (19.3 km) from the beach. The worst damage, however, occurred in New Orleans, Louisiana, hours after the storm passed. New Orleans, a well-loved city, is actually below sea level and protected by a series of levees that usually keep water out of the city.

The storm caused the levees to fail and 80 percent of the city flooded. Despite repeated warnings to evacuate before the storm arrived, many people were trapped in their houses during the flooding, with some drowning and others climbing to their roof waiting to be rescued. Because of slow rescue efforts, survivors told of seeing dead bodies float in the water for days before being collected. Because many of the people affected by the storm were poor and black, criticism of the federal government was loud.

Much of the blame fell on the Federal Emergency Management Agency (FEMA) and President George W. Bush for the slow response, although others criticized the state and local governments' uncoordinated response as well. Sharpton was quick to join the debate, leaving no doubt that he thought the color of the victims affected the rescue: "If we were not dealing with black people and poor people, we would not be dealing with this snail's pace reaction," he said, as quoted in an article in the *St. Petersburg Times*.

Even after the city was cleaned up, Sharpton, joined by the Reverend Jesse Jackson, pressured officials to allow displaced residents to vote in local elections. With so many homes destroyed in the flood—estimates said that fewer than half the city's 460,000 residents returned to their homes in the eight months after the tragedy—the two civil rights leaders held a rally, with about 2,000 supporters.

Sharpton even managed to find a New York connection to the event. Fifty families that had been evacuated from New Orleans were living at a hotel in Queens. After five months, even though the federal government was paying their tab, the hotel requested that these families leave. Sharpton helped lead a protest near the hotel, saying, "They are here because of government neglect. And they will not be evicted due to corporate insensitivity."

When filmmaker Spike Lee went to New Orleans to make a movie about the hurricane's effect on the city, the HBO documentary, *When the Levees Broke: A Requiem in Four Acts*, he named Sharpton and Mayor Ray Nagin of New Orleans as two of the heroes during the disaster.

HAITI

Long before an earthquake devastated Haiti in January 2010, Al Sharpton was already championing the plight of the poor people living there. So when the 7.0 magnitude earthquake struck about 16 miles (25.7 km) west of Port-au-Prince, the country's capital, Sharpton was ready to help.

He visited the area within days, traveling down on Martin Luther King Jr.'s birthday. "There will be no better way to say happy birthday to Martin Luther King," Sharpton was quoted as saying at the Haitian Consulate in Manhattan. "We all have some Haitian in us, and we stand in solidarity with the Haitian people until Haiti is restored."

DID YOU KNOW?

The Reverend Al Sharpton has been involved in many nonprofit organizations over the years. In 1991, he started a group called the National Action Network (NAN). On the group's Web site, NAN says it is one of the leading civil rights groups in the country: "NAN works within the spirit and tradition of Dr. Martin Luther King Jr. to promote a modern civil rights agenda that includes the fight for social justice and one standard of justice and decency for all people regardless of race, religion, national origin, and gender." The group was even formally incorporated as a nonprofit on April 4, 1994, the anniversary of King's assassination. As of 2010, the group had 25 employees and 25 chapters throughout the country. The group's motto, just like Sharpton's, is "No Justice, No Peace."

Of course, nothing ever seems simple in Sharpton's world, so it was unexpected when the *New York Post* reported in 2008 that his group received "boycott bucks" from corporations because the companies were afraid of negative publicity or product boycotts. Nearly 50 companies—including many major corporations such as Anheuser-Busch, Colgate-Palmolive, PepsiCo, General Motors, and Wal-Mart—have given thousands of dollars to Sharpton's charity or have paid to hire him as a consultant.

One General Motors spokesman said NAN had asked unsuccessfully for donations for six years. Then, when the company closed an African-American-owned dealership in the Bronx, New York, Sharpton boycotted GM's headquarters on Fifth Avenue. The following year, GM donated $5,000 to NAN. Sharpton also reportedly threatened PepsiCo with a consumer boycott in 1988, saying the company did not use African Americans in its ads. The company ended up

The mayor of New York, Michael Bloomberg, who visited the White House with Sharpton, warned him that going to the devastated land would do more harm than good. Bloomberg said the military was overwhelmed trying to aid residents, and he worried Sharpton would get in the way during his trip.

Sharpton's response was that he was going on a humanitarian mission, bringing doctors, equipment, and 80,000 gallons (302,832 liters) of water. Sharpton also teamed up with Haitian musician Wyclef Jean, a former member of the

putting the minister on its payroll for 10 years, paying him $25,000 a year as a consultant.

"I think this is quite clearly a shakedown operation," Peter Flaherty told the *Post*. Flaherty is president of the National Legal and Policy Center in Virginia, a conservative corporate watchdog. "[Sharpton is] good at harassing people and making noise. CEOs give him his way because it is a lot easier than confronting him."

The charges came as no surprise to Sharpton. He told the newspaper, "That's the old shakedown theory that the anti-civil-rights have used against us forever. Why can't they come up with one company that says that? No one has criticized me."

The group also has run into tax trouble, a frequent claim against Sharpton and his activities. In 2007, the New York State attorney general, Andrew Cuomo, whose father is a former governor of New York and a rival of Sharpton's, found that NAN failed to file financial reports for several years. The group was also said to owe the Internal Revenue Service, the country's tax-collection agency, $1.9 million in payroll taxes, according to the *Post* story.

Troubles aside, Sharpton expects NAN to be what he is remembered for. "My future is continuing to build an infrastructure for social justice [through this group]," Sharpton said in 2010. "I want to institutionalize the work, leave a social justice model like the NAACP [National Association for the Advancement of Colored People] did. That's where my legacy is, not running for office. If I can do that, that's what I want to do."

On April 1, 2006, Al Sharpton and Jesse Jackson lead a march across the Mississippi River Bridge in New Orleans, Louisiana. The two civil rights leaders called the protest to bring attention to the plight of Hurricane Katrina evacuees.

Fugees, who had started a nonprofit to help Haiti well before the earthquake. Both men took part in a pair of fundraising concert to help Haiti.

Sharpton also sharply criticized evangelist Pat Robertson, who said the earthquake was Haiti's punishment by God, because Haitians had made a deal with the devil to gain their freedom from the French in 1700s.

"To bring this kind of negative and wicked spirit into a scene where we are watching children's dead bodies stacked up is abominable to me," Sharpton said while preaching at the

Christ Universal Temple in Chicago's South Side. "This kind of foolishness, while people are laying in the rubble in Haiti fighting for their lives, shows a contempt some people have for the human condition."

An estimated 220,000 people were killed in the quake, with another 300,000 injured. One million people were thought to be homeless because an estimated 250,000 homes collapsed. Sharpton called for a long-term American commitment to the country as it rebuilds its infrastructure. On the NAN website, Sharpton wrote:

> I commend President Barack Obama for pledging $100 million in aid and the physical support of our troops to our Caribbean neighbor. The outpouring of money and relief pledges worldwide is a positive, motivating sign indeed. But the breadth and depth of destruction is beyond human comprehension, and we must work to ensure that such aid reaches those who need it the most. We must continue our efforts in the days, weeks, months and even years as time passes by; for the need will continue beyond today, and we must continue to act swiftly, thoroughly and without delay.

VIEQUES

While Sharpton has been arrested more than 20 times, most of these disorderly conduct charges carry little to no jail time or fines. When the reverend went to the Puerto Rican island of Vieques in 2001 to protest the Navy's test bombing there, however, the outcome stunned him and his supporters.

Most of the island of Vieques was purchased by the U.S. Navy in the 1940s, and since then it has been used as target practice for bombings and other military exercises. Critics say the decades of bombing have led to much higher-than-normal cancer rates for island dwellers. In 1999, island native and civilian employee of the U.S. Navy, David Sanes, was killed when two bombs fell 1.5 miles (2.4 km) away from their targets. Soon after, protests started where people illegally entered the practice grounds, with some of them camping there.

When Puerto Rican leaders asked Sharpton to help protest, he agreed and went to the island. Many celebrities joined the fight, including actor Edward James Olmos, lawyer Robert F. Kennedy Jr., and Guatemalan Nobel Prize winner Rigoberta Menchú.

When Sharpton was sentenced after his arrest, he received a 90-day sentence, longer than the others arrested with him, and much longer than earlier protesters. "I don't come from Puerto Rico," Sharpton told the judge, as quoted in a *New York Times* article. "But I am one for standing up for something that is right."

"All civil rights leaders understand they have to pay the penalty in the event that they exercise their civil rights,'" New York City Council Speaker Peter F. Vallone said. "But this is too severe a penalty."

Sharpton appealed the sentence to no avail. He went to a federal jail in New York with no cell phone, no entourage, and no way to get out early. These restrictions did not stop him from continuing his protest. Sharpton refused to eat solid food for 43 days, dropping 31 total pounds (14 kilograms).

After prison, he continued to watch his weight and continued to lose pounds. Estimates say Sharpton eventually lost 90 pounds (40.8 kg) from when he weighed approximately 300 pounds (136 kg). "Before Vieques, my diet was out of control," he said. "I ate whatever I wanted, whenever I wanted. I didn't exercise." Once he started losing weight, Sharpton realized how much better he felt. Even though he gained back some weight while running for president in 2004, he has since lost the weight and kept it off. Sharpton spends much of his time on the road, but admits that now he picks his hotel in part by rating its health center, noting that he works out in the morning before he reads the papers.

9

Amadou Diallo, Sean Bell, and Michael Jackson

So many times, the cases Al Sharpton has been involved in are like tinderboxes, ready to explode. Many times, Sharpton has been able to navigate through these dangerous waters, with some notable exceptions. The 1995 case of Freddie's Fashion Mart is one of those exceptions.

A building on 128th Street in Harlem was owned by a black church called United House of Prayer for All, which held gospel services on the second floor. The first floor held two tenants, Freddie's Fashion Mart and The Record Shack, a music store known for its vast collection of calypso, gospel, and jazz. Freddie's owner, Fred Harari, had a sublease that covered the record store. When Harari asked the record store to leave when its lease was up, the trouble started.

The record-store owner, Sikhulu Shange, complained, saying he was a model tenant who paid his rent on time and performed a valuable service for the neighborhood. His protests went to politicians and eventually included Sharpton. Picketers started showing up in front of the clothing store and Sharpton led some of the protests, one time telling the crowd, "We will not stand by and allow them to move this little brother so that some white interloper can expand his business." It was never clear whether the decision to close the record store came solely from Harari or from the African-American church that owned the building. Harari filed a civil lawsuit against the record store and Sharpton's National Action Network to try to stop the protests.

On December 8, 1995, just days before a hearing was scheduled, one of the protesters, Roland J. Smith, went into the clothing store with a gun and flammable liquid. He shot several customers, set the store on fire, and then fatally shot himself. Seven store employees died of smoke inhalation.

Although Sharpton later expressed regret for the "white" part of his interloper comment, he said the gunman was an open critic of his and his nonviolent efforts.

AMADOU DIALLO

The Diallo shooting better fit the model for most Sharpton cases—a tragic event that happens in a moment but reveals the racial tensions that simmer, usually just below the surface. This case, however, captured the attention of more than just Sharpton and his usual supporters, and before it was over, it showed Sharpton's power and his scheduling skills.

The incident started in the early morning of February 4, 1999, when Amadou Diallo, a 23-year-old Guinean immigrant, was coming home. Four plainclothes police officers were in the area, trying to catch a serial rapist. Plainclothes means the officers, all of whom were part of the city's Street Crimes Unit, were not wearing police uniforms because they wanted to investigate crimes without being easily identified as officers.

One of the policemen, who thought Diallo looked like the rapist, called for him to stop and put up his hands. Diallo ran up the steps to his apartment building and reached inside his coat. One of the officers thought he was reaching for a weapon, and he called "Gun!" to the fellow officers. The officers opened fire on the man, and during the shooting, one of the officers fell down the steps, appearing to be shot. The other three officers continued shooting.

The four officers ended up firing 41 bullets at Diallo, with 19 hitting and killing him. No weapon was found on Diallo; instead he was reaching for his wallet. A grand jury indicted all four officers with second-degree murder charges and reckless endangerment. The trial was moved to upstate New York to avoid the publicity that had enveloped the case.

The case touched off one of the biggest protests against police brutality and racial profiling ever seen. In the middle of it all was the Reverend Al Sharpton. He immediately began protests in front of One Police Plaza, New York City's police headquarters, to protest the shooting, the Special Crimes Unit, and Mayor Rudolph Giuliani. During the mayor's tenure, one of his biggest successes was drastically reducing the crime rate in the city, which made many people feel safer but made others question the aggressive tactics of his police department.

The protests started slowly, with eight people arrested the first day, 11 the second. With people horrified at an innocent man gunned down, however, more people started coming, including many famous people. In a story on a Trinity College Web site, Sharpton's role in the growing protest was described:

> As the protests grew, Sharpton served as the key broker.... Dave Saltonstall of the *Daily News* emphasized the wide variety of religious groups and people of social stature seeking to join the coalition: "All of them dialed the Rev. Al Sharpton and his National Action Network last week for a single reason: to learn how they, too, could get arrested in front of 1 Police Plaza to protest the police killing of Amadou Diallo."

Journalists were struck by the diversity of religious faiths and walks of life represented—a far, far broader group than had ever backed Sharpton's activism in the Tawana Brawley affair or the burning of Freddy's discount clothing store in Harlem. Sharpton became the outspoken voice in the media coverage and used the rhetoric of the Diallo case to move into the political and religious mainstream. News coverage portrayed him driving the protest.

When former Mayor Ed Koch called and asked Sharpton whether he could join the protests and get arrested, he asked to protest at 10 A.M. one Monday. Sharpton's reply: "I can't do it at 10, I can only do it at 11."

Sharpton himself told Jesse Jackson that the protests included blacks, Latinos, and whites united. Despite his past run-ins with members of the Jewish community, Sharpton was spotted marching with rabbis and shouting *shalom*, a Hebrew word meaning peace. Those arrested in Sharpton's protests included former Mayor David Dinkins, sitting U.S. Representative Charles Rangel, and State Comptroller H. Carl McCall, as well as actors and activists Dick Gregory, Ossie Davis, Rubie Dee, and Susan Sarandon, and Chloe Breyer, the daughter of Supreme Court Justice Stephen Breyer.

"When you look at the Diallo movement, probably since the South African apartheid movement, where have you seen people voluntarily going to jail—from housewives to ex-mayors—anytime in the last two decades," Sharpton said in our January 2010 interview. "Even in the '60s [during the civil rights movement] that didn't happen in New York. We had 13 consecutive days of people going to jail. That never happened."

The next year, a jury acquitted the four officers of all charges, touching off even more protests. In all, more than 1,700 people were arrested at police headquarters. While the criminal case was over, the impact of the actions continued.

On March 2, 2000, Al Sharpton led a demonstration outside the Department of Justice in Washington, D.C. to protest the verdict in the Amadou Diallo murder trial. From left are former Mayor David Dinkins of New York; Jackie Jackson, wife of Jesse Jackson; Sharpton; Diallo's father, Saikou Diallo; and NAACP President Kweisi Mfume.

Diallo's parents sued the city and the officers for violating their son's civil rights. The lawsuit asked for $61 million—$20 million plus $1 million for each shot fired. The family settled the suit for $3 million. In 2002, the Street Crimes Unit, discredited by the shooting, was disbanded.

The Diallo shooting continues to be referenced in many forms of art. More than 65 musicians have referred to it in song, with Bruce Springsteen releasing a song, "American Skin (41 Shots)," devoted solely to the event. It has also turned up in books and poetry, television shows and films, and even the work of a graffiti artist who sometimes tags his art with the words "41Shots."

SEAN BELL

As remarkable as the Diallo case seemed at the time, mixing together people's feeling about immigrants, police brutality, and the hot topic of racial profiling, seven years later another case repeated many of the same issues. The Sean Bell shooting also ended in the innocent death of an unarmed man shot by police.

On November 24, 2006, Bell went out with friends to celebrate his bachelor party at a club in Queens, New York. Bell and his two friends did not know, however, that the nightclub, Club Kalua, was under investigation by police for fostering prostitution. Seven officers, some in uniform and some not, were outside the club in the early morning hours when Bell and his friends went to leave.

The accounts of what happened next continue to be debated. An unidentified officer said he heard one of Bell's friends say, "Yo, get my gun," apparently in reference to an argument he had in the club. When a black undercover officer attempted to stop Bell, who was also black, before he drove off, Bell's car accelerated and hit the officer. The officer, Gescard Isnora, told his fellow officers that he thought he saw one of the car's occupants reach for a gun. He opened fire on the car and the others joined in, with a total of 50 bullets strafing the car in a span of seconds.

Bell was hit four times and killed. His friend Joseph Guzman was hit 19 times, and Trent Benefield, who was in the back seat, was hit three times. Both men ultimately survived the shootings.

The outrage was immediate. Sharpton and others called for a special prosecutor, but the case was given to a grand jury. Three of the five officers involved in the incident faced charges;

Isnora, who fired the first shot, and Michael Oliver, who fired 31 of the 50 shots, were charged with manslaughter, reckless endangerment, and assault. A third officer was charged with reckless endangerment. More than a year later, all three were acquitted of all the charges. Sharpton and the families involved immediately went to Bell's graveside for a memorial service.

Protests started anew, but this time Sharpton and the National Action Network tried a different tactic. While the Diallo protests were effective, Sharpton wanted more, so these protests reached out across the city. Sharpton and hundreds of others banded together to block the entrances to three New York City bridges. Sharpton was arrested with the two other shooting victims, Sean Bell's fiancé, and Bell's parents. Of the arrests, Sharpton said, "If you're not going to lock up the guilty in this town, I guess you have to lock up the innocent." Later protests tied up traffic at six key spots in the city, from House of the Lord Church in Brooklyn to 125th Street and Third Avenue in Harlem to One Police Plaza.

In a 2010 interview, Sharpton explained what facet of his protests most people did not understand. Sitting in a popular restaurant in midtown Manhattan, he said 90 percent of patrons would know who Sean Bell was more than three years after the shooting. If, however, you asked the same people who Omar Edwards was, most would not know, he said. Edwards was a police officer mistakenly shot to death by other police while he chased a suspect in 2009. People say Sharpton takes advantage of issues, but he said, "In many ways we create the issue.... There have been a lot of egregious acts, but unless someone builds and builds a movement around that, it's a one- or two-day story."

MICHAEL JACKSON

There were so many aspects to Michael Jackson's life and career that it often seems hard to believe they all fit into his 50 years. His career started with the Jackson 5, a group composed

Michael Jackson stands with Jesse Jackson and Al Sharpton at the end of a public viewing and funeral for James Brown in Augusta, Georgia, on December 30, 2006.

of him and four of his brothers. The group's first four singles went to No. 1 on the Billboard Hot 100 chart. He later segued into a solo career that included the top-selling record of all time, 1982's *Thriller,* which has sold more than 110 million copies. Of course, he was also known as a dancer so good and original that legendary dancer Fred Astaire not only praised him, but also asked Jackson to his house to teach him how to moonwalk.

Jackson was also known for his eccentricities, including his dramatic change in appearance and his multiple attempts to reshape his nose through plastic surgery. He was married twice, had three children, and was publicly accused twice of child molestation.

So it comes as little surprise that Jackson's humanitarian streak and respect of civil rights frequently went unnoticed. After his death in 2009, however, it was the Reverend Al Sharpton who delivered a moving eulogy to the entertainer. Sharpton reminded the television audience around the world that Jackson was human and that his fame and talent did much to advance the cause of African Americans in many ways, including breaking down barriers for blacks and making whites feel comfortable enough to not only watch Oprah Winfrey and Tiger Woods, but also to elect Barack Obama president.

Yet the first real meeting between Sharpton and Jackson came during a tense confrontation. Through his affiliation with James Brown, Sharpton had connections in the music business. When the Jackson family decided to reunite for a worldwide tour with Michael in 1984, Sharpton quickly noticed there was a lack of black promoters working with the family. He threatened with his best tool—a possible boycott of the tour.

The day after Sharpton held a news conference to make his concerns public, he found himself sitting in Jackson's house, surrounded by the Jackson family, including Michael, and each sibling's own manager. While negotiations about the tour occurred, Sharpton wrote that Michael sat on the floor playing with a balloon. Sharpton explained his vision for the tour, saying the family needed to give away free tickets to schools, colleges, and churches; make donations to worthy causes; and hire some poorer people to help be security at the shows. Sharpton recounted the incident in his book, writing, "In the middle of all this, Michael rolls up off the floor and says, 'I like that. He's right. We'll do it. But I want him to do it.' He pointed directly at me."

Because of the public nature of his complaints, and subsequent affiliation with the tour, some charged Sharpton with

IN HIS OWN WORDS

On July 7, 2009, at the Staples Center in Los Angeles, Al Sharpton gave a moving eulogy for Michael Jackson shown live around the world:

You would have to understand the journey of Michael to understand what he meant to all of us. He rose from a working-class family, with nothing but a dream. Michael never let the world turn him around from his dreams.... It was that dream that changed culture all over the world. When Michael started it was a different world. Because he kept going, he didn't accept limitations, he opened up the whole world. In the music business, he put on one glove, pulled his pants up, and broke down the color curtain where now our videos are shown and magazines put us on the cover. It was Michael Jackson that brought whites and blacks and Asians and Latinos together. It was Michael Jackson who made us sing "We are the World" and feed the hungry long before Live Aid. Because Michael Jackson kept going, he created a comfort level where people who felt they were separate, felt they were interconnected with his music. And it was that comfort level that kids from Japan and Ghana and France and Iowa and Pennsylvania got comfortable enough with each other where later it wasn't strange for us to watch Oprah on television, it wasn't strange to watch Tiger Woods golf. Those kids grew up from being teenage comfortable fans of Michael to being 40 years old and being comfortable to vote extorting the Jacksons so he could profit from them. Sharpton was investigated about this event, but no charges were ever filed.

Sharpton remained in touch with Jackson throughout his life, saying their bond came partly because both were approximately the same age, and because of Sharpton's involvement with Brown, both understood the craziness of the music business. In a 2010 interview, Sharpton said about Jackson, "He was a very shrewd businessman. He was keen on running his business, and not dying broke."

Jackson was sensitive to civil rights causes, but he did not want to be seen as a leader, Sharpton said, "which is why he came to me when he got in trouble" with the sexual assault

for a person of color to become president of the United States of America. Michael did that, Michael made us love each other, Michael taught us to stand with each other....

Don't focus on the scars, focus on the journey. Michael beat them. He rose to the top. He outsang his cynics. He outdanced his doubters, he outperformed the pessimists. Everytime he got knocked down, he got back up. Everytime you counted him out, he came back in. Michael never stopped. Michael never stopped. Michael never stopped.

I want to say to Mrs. Jackson, and Joe Jackson, his sisters and brothers. We thank you for giving us someone who taught us love and taught us hope. We know your heart is broken.... I hope the love that people are showing will make you know he didn't live in vain.

I want his three children to know. Wasn't nothing strange about your daddy. It was strange what your daddy had to deal with. But he dealt with it [standing ovation]. He dealt with it anyway, he dealt with it for us.

Some came today ... to say goodbye to Michael, I came to say thank you. Thank you because you never stopped. Thank you because you never gave up. Thank you because you never got out. Thank you 'cause you tore down our divisions. Thank you because you eradicated barriers. Thank you because you gave us hope. Thank you, Michael. Thank you, Michael. Thank you, Michael.

charges. The preacher also said that despite his fame and the adulation of fans around the globe, Jackson remained very sensitive and could get hurt by what people said about him. "A lot of people develop a thick skin," said Sharpton, who certainly has high tolerance for criticism about himself. "[Michael] never developed a thick skin."

Speaking about his eulogy, Sharpton said his goal during the speech was to humanize Michael Jackson and remind all of his fans and critics that underneath all the singing, dancing, fame, public criticism, and more, he was just an ordinary man. "I never thought to say anything to his kids," he added.

> I looked down and saw his kids, I knew I wanted to say something to [them]. What flashed in my mind was what would I say to my kids. I was speaking as a fellow traveler of Michael's of what I hoped someone would say for me. That's why it was so personal. Michael Jackson to me, was a product of his environment. He grew up around the world of Liberace [a flamboyant singer and piano player]. He wasn't strange. There was a context to who Michael was. People say Sharpton's flamboyant. In the aftermath of the civil rights movement, running around with James Brown, I'm a natural product of my environment.

10

Legacy

One of the hardest things for people to do is to judge someone's legacy or influence before his or her career ends. It is even harder to be objective when that person is yourself. Because the question of legacy has been constantly asked of the Reverend Al Sharpton, however, he has been answering these queries for years. For example, in 2001, when talking about his relationship with the Reverend Jesse Jackson, Sharpton said, "I'm still learning to have a father figure, and Jesse is still learning how to deal with a rebellious son. We're working on it."

Two years earlier, Sharpton discussed his legacy while answering yet another question about his hair and whether he regretted allowing a photographer to take what became a famous photo of him getting his hair styled. Dwight Garner of *Salon* asked him, "You must get tired about talking about your 'do." "Yeah, I do," Sharpton replied.

I've always had the feeling that people who are only hair-deep in their analysis are so trivial that I don't let them bother me. Lately I've found myself thinking more about how people judge this time historically—not how it's seen in the daily papers. And 50 years from now, people won't remember how I wore my hair or what clothes I wore. Fifty years from now, whether my critics like it or not, people will say I put race on the front burner and got some things done. All of my personality flaws and my style won't matter. I made some changes happen. Many black kids are killed, but the reason people will remember Howard Beach or Bensonhurst is that we built a movement around it. It's not like these are the only incidents. History will have to say whether it's all meant anything. I may not be of King's stature, but I am in his tradition.

SELF-AWARENESS

Sharpton's self-awareness, his understanding of not only the media but why some people like him while others deplore him, sets him apart from most public figures. He is at ease both poking fun at himself, including for his hair and appearance, and having others tease him. He summed up the reason for this when asked about Jesse Jackson once:

I'm not as sensitive to critics as he is. I grew up with James Brown and Don King [a boxing promoter], and they were getting attacked all the time. I came up expecting controversy. But Jesse's mentor had the Nobel Peace Prize and universal acclamation by the time Jesse went to work for him. He expects to be treated the way Dr. King was, and I expect to be treated like Don King.

Some things, however, Sharpton has no sense of humor for—most notably, fair-weather civil rights supporters. Speaking to about 150 people in the House of Justice auditorium at the headquarters of Sharpton's National Action Network in Harlem in 2002, he said:

> This is real. This ain't no part-time, do-it-when-you-like-it, I'm black today, having a black attack, then I'm going back to normal tomorrow. Many of you at home get black attacks. Well, cop stopped the car, so we're mad. So you go to two rallies. Let me tell you something. What we can't convince you of by preaching, the forces are going to force you into.

Sharpton is also very serious about maintaining nonviolent marches: "We never had any violence in any of our marches, except when the guy stabbed me." While critics would point to cases such as Freddie's Fashion Mart, during which a protester killed people, or some of the riots where Jews were killed or beaten, Sharpton is clear in saying these incidents did not happen during his marches. "To have marches where people are throwing stuff at us, to be able to keep people's heads on is not easy," he said in 2010. "Mrs. King [Coretta Scott King, the widow of Martin Luther King Jr.] would always mention that."

Talking about one of the Sean Bell marches he led, where about 50,000 protesters walked down Fifth Avenue in Manhattan on the Saturday before Christmas, Sharpton explained how hard it was to control everyone. Because one of the people shot alongside Bell was close to some gang members, there were plenty of gang members marching that day

> I don't think people understand the organizing, and the manpower, and the structure you need to pull these things [off]. To keep [these gang members] from even grabbing a bag is a task.... All you have to do, if people think I'm embellishing it, is ask yourself how come other people aren't able to pull off those numbers. If it's so easy to do it, why isn't anybody else doing it?

While Sharpton gets criticized for taking so many cases, he says no one knows how many he turns down. Since his 40-market radio show started in 2006, the number of people seeking his help has increased dramatically. The National Action Network and its 25 employees help him vet cases thoroughly before getting involved. He noted: "I'm definitely more cautious. We get everything from legitimate cases to kooks [just] because we're out there. It's hard to go through the sorting process."

DID YOU KNOW?

Al Sharpton has made his career by making his own decisions and not being afraid to surprise people, whether by hosting *Saturday Night Live*, running against an incumbent Democratic senator, or just agreeing to appear on TV shows hosted by conservative pundits. So when President Barack Obama invited Sharpton to visit him at the White House after his election, Sharpton had another surprise up his sleeve.

A year earlier, Sharpton had written some columns about education that a former speaker of the House of Representatives, Newt Gingrich, had let him know that he admired. Gingrich, a Republican who was a bitter rival of President Bill Clinton when he was in the White House, is not generally liked in Democratic Party circles.

Gingrich invited Sharpton to speak at a Republican group, and both were surprised when Sharpton got two or three standing ovations. Sharpton returned the favor and invited Gingrich to speak at his National Action Network conference. Gingrich was well received. So when Obama's office asked Sharpton who he would like to bring to his meeting, he said, "Let's make it bipartisan, invite Gingrich" and Mayor Michael Bloomberg of New York. Gingrich and Sharpton continued to share views on education. Finding some common ground with the president, the two—with Department of Education Secretary Arne Duncan—decided to hold a series of school visits and media events to highlight some of the needed changes in public education.

The trio visited Philadelphia, New Orleans, and Baltimore to try to push the cities to repair their failing school systems. All three men are in favor of adding charter schools to inner cities. Charters are schools that get public

OUTSIDE ANALYSIS

When trying to draw an accurate picture of Sharpton, it is helpful to listen to outside voices as well. Percy Sutton, a long-time friend who was also Manhattan borough president for a time, recalled the talents of the young preacher: "He was an assembler of information and knowledge. He ingested material, and—how shall I say it?—regurgitated it much enhanced. Many people sort of adopted him, because they wanted to share with him."

education funding, but follow fewer rules as they try new methods to improve the education delivered.

Interviewed on NBC's *Today* show, Gingrich and Sharpton were asked how they had agreed to work together on education in view of the many differences they have had on other issues. "I think that he has it exactly right, that education has to be the No. 1 civil right of the 21st century and I've been passionate about reforming education," Gingrich said. "And we can't get it done as a partisan issue."

Sharpton said the time has come to "change the conversation ... to say we need to put everybody's hands on the table." He said he believes that "if there's anything Americans should be mature enough about to have a decent conversation, it's the education of their children."

On NBC's *Meet the Press*, Sharpton added, "We are going backwards in a technological age as a country, and in my community we're getting inexperienced teachers, unequal education. So if this means that we have to come together and make alliances to deal with the fact that almost half of the young people in my community are not even getting a high school diploma, I think the president is right."

Sharpton says that he and Gingrich did argue while on the road together, but mostly about health care reform. "He understands being outside the box," Sharpton said. "I think it comes down to, do you believe what you're saying and ignore the criticism. Newt is very smart. I knew he was all right, but he knows some history. Now he comes almost all the time to the wrong conclusions, but the buildup is great. It's a great multiplication example, but the wrong answer."

On May 7, 2009, President Barack Obama meets in the Oval Office at the White House in Washington, D.C. with *(from left)* Mayor Michael Bloomberg of New York, the Reverend Al Sharpton, and former Speaker of the House Newt Gingrich to discuss education reform.

Asked about the ability to speak off the cuff and not follow written speeches, Sharpton refers to his start: "I was preaching so young, I grew up learning how to think on my feet. With a more expansive organization [now], I might run something by them, but my instincts are still the same. Civil rights is having to deal with seizing an issue at the time. A lot of it you have to do on your feet."

As always with Sharpton, there is an opposing viewpoint to consider. While he was getting praise for his initial role in the Diallo shooting, he also called for the four officers involved to be charged even before the grand jury was finished listening to evidence. Michael Myers, the director of the New York Civil Rights Coalition, said, "You cannot regard someone as a civil rights activist who does not believe in the process of law."

PRESIDENT BARACK OBAMA

Maybe the best way to judge Sharpton is to consider the tricky balancing act he faced when Senator Barack Obama was running for president in 2008. Because Sharpton was the dominant African-American candidate in 2004, he did draw news stories when he officially announced he would not run in 2008. Given that he was not a serious contender in 2008 and Obama was, however, this switch was less like passing the torch than a smooth transferal of trying to show his supporters he approved of Obama, without being so strong in his support that his opponents automatically turned against Obama too.

One incident during the campaign helped start their relationship. Sharpton recalls that someone tried to get both him and Obama to speak at a political seminar on race. Obama's people were concerned, so the candidate picked up the phone and called Sharpton. He said it would not help him to be forced into such an event. Sharpton thought about solutions and called him back, and he said, "I tell you what, I won't come." Obama said he was not asking Sharpton not to attend. Sharpton, however, was smart enough to realize it was better for him not to attend. The incident never occurred, and the issue of Sharpton's support for Obama and Obama's feelings on racial issues did not become a news story. "We developed a relationship," Sharpton recalled. "He came to Sylvia's [a world-famous soul food restaurant located in the heart of Harlem] and made a big splash. He made it very clear that he was going to relate to me. That he wasn't me, and I wasn't him."

LOOKING FORWARD

At various times, Sharpton has listed some of his proudest accomplishments, citing his campaign against racial profiling in the Sean Bell case, or his strong run for New York City mayor in 1997. When he was asked why he did not pursue more concrete goals, however, he was clear: "I have no desire to be an inside player, and no desire to be in social service. Building housing is good. But I'll support Johnny Ray Youngblood [a Brooklyn minister] in doing that. I do social change—broad, policy climate setting. And that's what I'll always do."

While this work is a source of pride, it is also an obligation he must uphold. Sharpton said he remembers coming back from his first trip to Africa in 1994. He was met at the airport by a woman who told him her unarmed brother had been choked to death by police in Staten Island. He recalled:

> From one of the highest points of my career and a world-historical triumph for blacks to "Here we go again." It reminded me of what Frederick Douglass [a former slave who fought tirelessly for equal rights in the 1800s] said, "Life is a struggle and the struggle is your life." You can never sit back and think it's over. Every day . . . I've been on the front line of the movement, and I haven't had time until now to even pause and reflect, because I have to get up every day ready for war, and I go to bed every night thanking God that I made it one more day.

Asked in 2010 about his legacy and also his future, Sharpton said, "If history says, in my generation, I kept the banner of social justice and civil rights going, that would be fine with me." Speaking about his future, he added, "I'm not on the decline, I'm almost to where I'm leveling off my flight, not declining for arrival. That's not happening no time soon."

1954 Alfred Charles Sharpton Jr. is born on October 3 in Brooklyn, New York.

1958 Sharpton gives his first sermon at the age of four at Washington Temple Church of God in Christ.

1963 Sharpton's father and half-sister move out of the house when it is revealed they are having an affair; Sharpton moves with his mother to Brooklyn and the family goes on welfare.

1964 Sharpton is licensed and ordained as a Pentecostal minister.

1965 Sharpton meets Adam Clayton Powell Jr., a charismatic preacher from Harlem; the two would be friends until Powell's death.

1968 The 13-year-old preacher meets 26-year-old Jesse Jackson when he starts working for an organization that helps black families; Jackson becomes a mentor to the teen and their relationship endures for decades.

1973 The preacher meets soul singer James Brown, who becomes a father figure to Sharpton, and even influences the young man's famous hairstyle.

1985 Sharpton becomes involved in the Bernhard Goetz case, calling for the white gunman to receive a harsher penalty for shooting four black youths in a subway car.

1986 Sharpton takes his biggest civil rights case yet when a black youth is killed in Howard Beach, Queens.

1987 Black teen Tawana Brawley is found in a trash bin outside New York, and she says she was held hostage for four days and sexually abused by white men; Sharpton and others come to her defense, refusing to apologize when she is found to have fabricated her story.

1989 Sharpton is arrested on suspicion of stealing money from his nonprofit group and evading state taxes; he beats all charges. After another black young man is killed in a racial incident, Sharpton marches through Bensonhurst, Brooklyn, to raise awareness; Sharpton is stabbed with a steak knife as he readies the twenty-ninth march in Bensonhurst; he spends less than a week in the hospital and recovers in two months.

1991   A seven-year-old black boy is hit and killed by a car in a Jewish motorcade; riots engulf Crown Heights, Brooklyn, and blacks stab a Jew in retaliation, killing him; Sharpton tries to sue the driver of the car but is thwarted; Sharpton starts his own nonprofit organization, the National Action Network.

1992   Sharpton tries his first run at national office, entering the Democratic primary for U.S. senator; he loses the four-way race but garners more support than expected.

1994   Sharpton runs for Senate again, this time opposing incumbent Democrat Daniel Patrick Moynihan; he loses again but garners an even larger percentage of the vote than in 1992; he travels to Rwanda to visit refugee camps and publicize the genocide taking place in that part of Africa; he becomes a Baptist.

1995   When a black tenant is threatened with eviction from a clothing store owned by a Jewish man, Sharpton rallies to his cause; later another protester enters the clothing store, shooting people and starting a fire; seven people and the gunman die.

1996   Sharpton publishes his first autobiography, *Go and Tell Pharaoh.*

1997   Sharpton runs for mayor of New York City, nearly forcing a Democratic runoff with eventual candidate Ruth Messinger.

1999   Unarmed immigrant Amadou Diallo is shot at by police 41 times, killing him; Sharpton leads protests that end with 1,700 people being arrested, including two former mayors; Sharpton protests the U.S. Navy bombings on the Puerto Rican island of Vieques; he receives a 90-day jail sentence; goes on a liquid diet for 43 days, losing 31 pounds.

2002 Sharpton publishes his second autobiography, *Al on America*.

2003 Sharpton decides to run for president as one of 10 candidates hoping to oppose President George W. Bush in the general election; despite poor support, he stays in the race until Senator John Kerry wins the party's nomination; late in the year he hosts *Saturday Night Live*, poking fun at his reputation.

2004 Sharpton gives a prime-time speech at the Democratic National Convention, criticizing President George W. Bush.

2005 Hurricane Katrina rips into the Gulf Coast; Sharpton argues for the rights of the poor, black families who have lost their homes in the tragedy.

2006 Unarmed Sean Bell is shot and killed by police as he leaves his bachelor party in Queens; protests led by Sharpton tie up traffic at key points in New York for several days; Sharpton's radio show, *Keepin' It Real with Al Sharpton*, debuts.

2009 Sharpton gives a eulogy at singer Michael Jackson's public funeral in Los Angeles; Sharpton and former Speaker of the House Newt Gingrich meet President Barack Obama in the Oval Office; the two later go on a tour of schools to try to improve urban education.

2010 Sharpton flies to Haiti in the days following a devastating earthquake, bringing doctors and supplies to the poor country.

Branch, Taylor. *Parting the Waters: America in the King Years 1954–63*. New York: Simon & Schuster, 1989.

Frady, Marshall. *Jesse: The Life and Pilgrimmage of Jesse Jackson*. New York: Simon & Schuster, 2006.

Mandery, Evan J., R.J. Matson, and Rob Shepperson. *The Campaign: Rudy Giuliani, Ruth Messinger, Al Sharpton, and the Race to Be Mayor of New York City*. Boulder, Col.: Westview Press, 1999.

McFadden, Robert D. *Outrage: The Story Behind the Tawana Brawley Hoax*. New York: Bantam, 1990.

Sabato, Larry J. *Divided States of America: The Slash and Burn Politics of the 2004 Presidential Election*. London: Longman Publishing Group, 2005.

Sharpton Al, and Anthony Walton. *Go and Tell Pharaoh: The Autobiography of The Reverend Al Sharpton*. New York: Doubleday, 1996.

Sharpton Al, with Karen Hunter. *Al on America*. New York: Dafina Books, Kensington Publishing Corp., 2002.

Taraborrelli, J. Randy. *Michael Jackson: The Magic, The Madness, The Whole Story, 1958–2009*. New York: Hachette Book Group, 2009.

WEB SITES

"A Defiant Sharpton Vows Not to Apologize," *New York Times*
http://www.nytimes.com/1998/07/19/nyregion/a-defiant-sharpton
-vows-not-to-apologize.html

National Action Network
http://www.nationalactionnetwork.net/

"The People's Preacher," *New Yorker*
http://archives.newyorker.com/?i=2002-02-18#folio=156

"The Post-Sharpton Sharpton," *New York Times*
http://www.nytimes.com/2001/03/18/magazine/the-post
-sharpton-sharpton.html?scp=1&sq=The%20Post-Sharpton%
20Sharpton&st=cse

"The Race-Baiter in the Campaign," *Boston Globe*
http://www.boston.com/news/globe/editorial_opinion/oped/
articles/2003/11/09/the_race_baiter_in_the_campaign/

The Reverend Al Sharpton, *New York Times*
http://topics.nytimes.com/top/reference/timestopics/people/s/
al_sharpton/index.html?scp=1-spot&sq=al%20sharpton&st=cse

"Rev vs. Rev," *New York*
http://nymag.com/nymetro/news/politics/national/2004race/5570/

"Sharpton, Gingrich, Duncan Team Up on School Reforms," *USA Today*
http://www.usatoday.com/news/education/2009-08-14-sharpton
-gingrich_N.htm

"Sharpton and 3 From Bronx Are Jailed in Vieques Protest," *New York Times*
http://www.nytimes.com/2001/05/24/nyregion/sharpton-and
-3-from-bronx-are-jailed-in-vieques-protest.html?pagewanted=2

"Tawana Brawley," *New York Times*
http://topics.nytimes.com/topics/reference/timestopics/people/b/
tawana_brawley/index.html?offset=15&

Picture Credits

Wayne D'Orio is an award-winning writer and editor who has worked for a variety of newspapers and magazines throughout his career. He has spent 10 years covering education for various publications, including *Scholastic Administrator*, and has written a biography of Carol Moseley Braun. He lives in Connecticut with his wife and two children.